THE ENLIGHTENED MIND

Also by Stephen Mitchell

POETRY
Parables and Portraits

TRANSLATIONS
Variable Directions: The Selected Poetry of Dan Pagis
Tao Te Ching
The Book of Job
The Selected Poetry of Yehuda Amichai (with Chana Bloch)
The Sonnets to Orpheus
The Lay of the Love and Death of Cornet Christoph Rilke
Letters to a Young Poet
The Notebooks of Malte Laurids Brigge
The Selected Poetry of Rainer Maria Rilke

ANTHOLOGIES
The Enlightened Heart: An Anthology of Sacred Poetry
Dropping Ashes on the Buddha:
The Teaching of Zen Master Seung Sahn

FOR CHILDREN
The Creation (with paintings by Ori Sherman)

BOOKS ON TAPE
The Enlightened Heart
Letters to a Young Poet
Parables and Portraits
Tao Te Ching
The Book of Job
Selected Poems of Rainer Maria Rilke

THE
ENLIGHTENED
MIND

An Anthology of Sacred Prose

Edited by Stephen Mitchell

HarperCollins*Publishers*

FIRST EDITION

Designer: David Bullen
Compositor: Wilsted & Taylor

Copyright acknowledgments begin on page 225.

Library of Congress Cataloging-in-Publication Data
The Enlightened mind : an anthology of sacred prose /
edited by Stephen Mitchell. — 1st ed.
    p.   cm.
  Includes bibliographical references.
  ISBN 0-06-016528-6
  1. Religious literature, English.   I. Mitchell,
Stephen, 1943–
BL29.E54 1991
291.8—dc20   90-55936

---

91 92 93 94 95 CW 10 9 8 7 6 5 4 3 2 1

To my parents-in-law,
Mayo and Shao-Cheng (Shelton) Chang

CONTENTS

FOREWORD

The modern Indian sage Ramana Maharshi once defined a genuine seeker as someone who has "a constant and passionate longing to break free from life's sorrow—not by running away from it, but by growing beyond his mind and by experiencing in himself the reality of the Self, which knows neither birth nor death." Longing is, for most of us, an essential stage in spiritual life.

But it is only a stage, an arrow that points inward, to the experience of God. It is not the experience itself, just as seeking is not finding, although we must seek in order to find. And if we seek the kingdom of heaven anywhere else ("It is here!"; "It is there!"), how can we realize that it is truly here? "*Reality* and *perfection*," Spinoza said, "are synonymous."

This anthology and its companion volume, *The Enlightened Heart*, collect the poetry and prose not of longing but of fulfillment. The men and women who speak to us from these pages have each, to a greater or lesser extent, entered the kingdom of heaven. In order to tell us about what is unknown and unknowable, they have to speak in terms of the known. That is why metaphorical language is so indispensable, and why the distinction between poetry and prose finally breaks down.

The distinction between heart and mind is just as artificial; Chinese, for example, has only one word for our two. So I hereby retract *Mind* in *The Enlightened Mind*, and *Prose* in *An Anthology of Sacred Prose*. And come to think of it, I would also like to retract *Enlightened*. (The Buddha said, "Please don't think that when I attained enlightenment, there was anything I attained.") As for *Sacred*: "Throw away sacredness and wisdom," Lao-tzu said, "and people will be a hundred times happier."

What are we left with? Let's just say that this book is a testimony of those who have seen God's face in the mirror, a collection of good words from the kingdom of here and now: much ado about Nothing.

THE
ENLIGHTENED
MIND

The first four sentences of this first selection are an epitome of all spiritual teaching, a sword to cut through the Gordian knot of theodicy, and a great delight. As for the Self: call it Self, God, Buddha; say that it is everywhere, say that it is nowhere; describe it as darkness or as light: it doesn't matter. What matters is to taste and see.

That is perfect. This is perfect. Perfect comes from perfect. Take perfect from perfect, the remainder is perfect.

May peace and peace and peace be everywhere.

Whatever lives is full of the Lord. Claim nothing; enjoy, do not covet His property.

Then hope for a hundred years of life doing your duty. No other way can prevent deeds from clinging, proud as you are of your human life.

The Self is one. Unmoving, it moves faster than the mind. The senses lag, but Self runs ahead. Unmoving, it outruns pursuit. Out of Self comes the breath that is the life of all things.

Unmoving, it moves; is far away, yet near; within all, outside all.

Of a certainty the man who can see all creatures in himself, himself in all creatures, knows no sorrow.

How can a wise man, knowing the unity of life, seeing all creatures in himself, be deluded or sorrowful?

The Self is everywhere, without a body, without a shape, whole, pure, wise, all knowing, far shining, self-depending, all transcending; in the eternal procession assigning to every period its proper duty.

Translated by W. B. Yeats and Shree Purohit Swami

The Self is the ear of the ear, the eye of the eye. It is the mind of the mind, the speech of speech, and the life of life. Not clinging to any of the senses, not attached to any thought in the mind, the wise become one with the deathless Self.

Eye cannot see It, tongue cannot utter It, mind cannot grasp It. There is no way to learn or to teach It. It is different from the known, beyond the unknown. In this all the ancient Masters agree.

That which makes the tongue speak but which cannot be spoken by the tongue—that alone is God, not what people worship.

That which makes the mind think but which cannot be thought by the mind—that alone is God, not what people worship.

That which makes the eye see but which cannot be seen by the eye—that alone is God, not what people worship.

That which makes the ear hear but which cannot be heard by the ear—that alone is God, not what people worship.

If you think that you know God, you know very little; all that you can know are ideas and images of God.

I do not know God, nor can I say that I don't know It. If you understand the meaning of "I neither know nor don't know," you understand God.

Those who realize that God cannot be known, truly know; those who claim that they know, know nothing. The ignorant think that God can be grasped by the mind; the wise know It beyond knowledge.

When you see that God acts through you at every moment, in every movement of mind or body, you attain true freedom. When you realize the truth, and cling to nothing in the world, you enter eternal life.

"The whole of wisdom," said Ramana Maharshi, *"is contained in two Biblical statements: 'I am that* I am' *and 'Be still and know that I am God.'"*

And God looked at everything that he had made, and behold, it was very good.

———

Jacob was left alone; and a being wrestled with him until daybreak. And when he saw that he could not defeat him, he touched the hollow of his thigh; and the hollow of Jacob's thigh was out of joint, as he wrestled with him. And he said, "Let me go, for daybreak has come." And Jacob said, "I will not let you go until you bless me." And he said, "Your name will no longer be Jacob, but Israel: for you have wrestled with God, and have won." And Jacob said, "Please, tell me your name." And he said, "Why do you want to know my name?" And he blessed him there. And Jacob called the place Peniel: "for I have seen God face to face, and my life has been saved."

———

Moses said, "When I tell the people that the God of their fathers has sent me, they will ask his name. What shall I tell them?" And God said, "*I am what I am.* Tell them that *I am* has sent you."

———

"You shall love the Unnamable with all your heart and with all your mind and with all your strength. And these words which I command you today shall be upon your heart; and you shall teach them to your children, and speak of them when you sit in your house and when you walk on the road and when you lie down and when you rise up; and you shall bind them as a sign upon your hand and they shall be like a pendant between your eyes; and you shall write them upon the doorposts of your house and upon your gates."

———

"Love your neighbor as yourself."

———

For this pattern which I give you today is not hidden from you, and is not far away. It is not in heaven, for you to say, "Who will go up to heaven and bring it down for us, so that we can hear it and do it?" Nor is it beyond the sea, for you to say, "Who will cross the sea and bring it back for us, so that we can hear it and do it?" But the teaching is very near you, it is in your mouth and in your heart, so that you can do it.

———

And he said, "Go and stand on the mountain before the Unnamable." And behold, the Unnamable passed by, and a great wind tore the mountains and shattered the rocks; but the Unnamable was not in the wind. And after the wind, an earthquake; but the Unnamable was not in the earthquake. And after the earthquake, a fire; but the Unnamable was not in the fire. And after the fire, a still, small voice.

———

"I form light and create darkness; I make peace and create evil."

———

"I have put my truth in your innermost mind, and I have written it in your heart. No longer does a man need to teach his brother about God. For all of you know Me, from the most ignorant to the most learned, from the poorest to the most powerful."

———

God has made everything beautiful in its time, and has put eternity in our heart.

———

"Be still, and know that I am God."

———

You have hidden the truth in darkness; through this mystery you teach me wisdom.

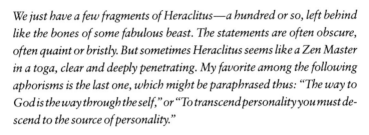

We just have a few fragments of Heraclitus—a hundred or so, left behind like the bones of some fabulous beast. The statements are often obscure, often quaint or bristly. But sometimes Heraclitus seems like a Zen Master in a toga, clear and deeply penetrating. My favorite among the following aphorisms is the last one, which might be paraphrased thus: "The way to God is the way through the self," or "To transcend personality you must descend to the source of personality."

All things flow.

———

The sun is new every day.

———

Opposition brings together, and from discord comes perfect harmony.

———

From all, one; and from one, all.

———

You can't step twice into the same river.

———

You won't discover the limits of the soul, however far you go.

———

Eternity is a child playing checkers.

———

The hidden harmony is better than the obvious one.

———

It is in change that things find rest.

———

To men, some things are good and some are bad. But to God, all things are good and beautiful and just.

———

The way up and the way down are one and the same.

———○———

"Buddha" means "the awakened one"—that is, someone who has woken up from the dream of being a separate ego in a material universe. Gautama Siddhartha, whom we affectionately, ridiculously, call the Buddha, taught for forty-five years. In all those years, and in all the hundreds of thousands of teaching words that he uttered, his message was simply this: "You are all Buddhas. There is nothing that you need to achieve. Just open your eyes."

It is proper to doubt. Do not be led by holy scriptures, or by mere logic or inference, or by appearances, or by the authority of religious teachers. But when you realize that something is unwholesome and bad for you, give it up. And when you realize that something is wholesome and good for you, do it.

———

As a mother at the risk of her life watches over her only child, so let everyone cultivate a boundlessly compassionate mind toward all beings.

———

When you see the unborn, uncreated, unconditioned, you are liberated from everything born, created, and conditioned.

———

A man walking along a highroad sees a great river, its near bank dangerous and frightening, its far bank safe. He collects sticks and foliage, makes a raft, paddles across the river, and reaches the other shore. Now suppose that, after he reaches the other shore, he takes the raft and puts it on his head and walks with it on his head wherever he goes. Would he be using the raft in an appropriate way? No;

a reasonable man will realize that the raft has been very useful to him in crossing the river and arriving safely on the other shore, but that once he has arrived, it is proper to leave the raft behind and walk on without it. This is using the raft appropriately.

In the same way, all truths should be used to cross over; they should not be held on to once you have arrived. You should let go of even the most profound insight or the most wholesome teaching; all the more so, unwholesome teachings.

———

Be a lamp to yourself. Be your own confidence. Hold to the truth within yourself, as to the only truth.

———

Tzu-ssu was Confucius' grandson; tradition ascribes to him The Central Harmony, *the second of the four Confucian classics, from which the following passages are taken. The central figure in this treatise is "the mature person," mature spiritually, emotionally, and ethically, in every situation acting with grace, dignity, and compassion. How civilized these ancient Chinese are! There is nothing here that Thomas Jefferson couldn't have embraced with his whole heart.*

What is bestowed by heaven is called human nature. The fulfillment of human nature is called the Tao. The cultivation of the Tao is called true learning.

The Tao is the law of nature, which you can't depart from even for one instant. If you could depart from it, it wouldn't be the Tao. Thus the mature person looks into his own heart and respects what is unseen and unheard. Nothing is more manifest than the hidden; nothing is more obvious than the unseen. Thus the mature person pays attention to what is happening in his inmost self.

Before pleasure, anger, sorrow, and joy have arisen, we are in the center. When these passions have arisen and when all attain their proper degree, we are in harmony. That center is the root of the universe; that harmony is the Tao, reaching out to all things. Once we find the center and achieve harmony, heaven and earth take their proper places, and all things are fully nourished.

———

The Book of Songs says,
> The hawk soars to the heavens,
> the fish plunges to the depths.

This means that there is no place where the Tao doesn't penetrate. For the mature person, the Tao begins in the relation between man and woman, and ends in the infinite vastness of the universe.

Confucius said, "To find the Tao, there is nowhere you need to search. If it is not inside you, it is not the Tao." The Book of Songs says,

> When you carve an axe handle,
> the model is near at hand.

In making the handle of an axe by cutting wood with an axe, the model is indeed near at hand. Thus, in dealing with people, we already have the perfect model of behavior inside us. Just act sincerely, in accordance with your true nature. Don't do to others what you wouldn't want done to you.

———

The mature person accepts his situation and doesn't desire anything outside it. If he finds himself rich and honored, he acts as a rich man should act; if he is poor, he acts as a poor man should act; if he is among barbarians, he acts as a barbarian should act; if he is in trouble, he acts as someone in trouble should act. Life can present him with no situation in which he isn't master of himself.

In a high position, he doesn't domineer over his subordinates; in a low position, he doesn't fawn on his superiors. He makes sure that his own conduct is correct and seeks nothing from others; thus he is never disappointed. He has no complaints against heaven and no blame toward other people.

Therefore the mature person lives in perfect serenity, awaiting the decrees of heaven, while the unworthy person walks on the edge of danger, always trying to keep one step ahead of his fate.

Confucius said, "In the archer there is a resemblance to the mature person. When he misses the bull's-eye, he turns and seeks the reason for his failure in himself."

———

Confucius said, "Sincerity is the way of heaven; arriving at sincerity is the way of man. The sincere person does the right thing without trying, understands the truth without thinking, and acts always in keeping with the Tao."

Only those who have absolute sincerity can fulfill their own nature. Fulfilling their own nature, they can fulfill the nature of other people. Fulfilling the nature of other people, they can fulfill the nature of all beings. Fulfilling the nature of all beings, they can participate in the transforming and nourishing powers of heaven and earth.

Sincerity is the fulfillment of our own nature, and to arrive at it we need only follow our true self. Sincerity is the beginning and end of existence; without it, nothing can endure. Therefore the mature person values sincerity above all things.

Sincerity is not only the fulfillment of our own being; it is also the quality through which all beings are fulfilled. When we fulfill our own being, we become truly human; when we fulfill all beings, we arrive at true understanding. These qualities—humanity and understanding—are inherent in our nature, and by means of them we unite the inner and the outer. Thus, when we act with sincerity, everything we do is right.

The first of the following selections is from Socrates' famous culminating speech in the Symposium. *Most of the speech is a long quotation from his teacher, Diotima; he prefaces it by saying, "I want to talk about some lessons I was once given by a Mantinean woman named Diotima—a woman deeply versed in this and in many other fields of knowledge. She is the one who brought about a ten years' postponement of the great plague of Athens on the occasion of a certain sacrifice, and she is the one who taught me the philosophy of love."*

The second passage is the conclusion of the Phaedrus: *one of the most charming, most complete prayers ever uttered.*

"Whoever has been initiated so far in the mysteries of Love and has viewed all these aspects of the beautiful in due succession, is at last drawing near the final revelation. And now, Socrates, there bursts upon him that wondrous vision which is the very soul of the beauty he has toiled so long for. It is an everlasting loveliness which neither comes nor goes, which neither flowers nor fades, for such beauty is the same on every hand, the same then as now, here as there, this way as that way, the same to every worshipper as it is to every other.

"Nor will his vision of the beautiful take the form of a face, or of hands, or of anything that is of the flesh. It will be neither words, nor knowledge, nor a something that exists in something else, such as a living creature, or the earth, or the heavens, or anything that is— but subsisting of itself and by itself in an eternal oneness, while every lovely thing partakes of it in such sort that, however much the parts may wax and wane, it will be neither more nor less, but still the same inviolable whole.

"And so, when his prescribed devotion to boyish beauties has carried our candidate so far that the universal beauty dawns upon his inward sight, he is almost within reach of the final revelation.

And this is the way, the only way, he must approach, or be led toward, the sanctuary of Love. Starting from individual beauties, the quest for the universal beauty must find him ever mounting the heavenly ladder, stepping from rung to rung—that is, from one to two, and from two to every lovely body, from bodily beauty to the beauty of institutions, from institutions to learning, and from learning in general to the special lore that pertains to nothing but the beautiful itself—until at last he comes to know what beauty is.

"And if, my dear Socrates," Diotima went on, "man's life is ever worth the living, it is when he has attained this vision of the very soul of beauty. And once you have seen it, you will never be seduced again by the charm of gold, of dress, of comely boys, or lads just ripening to manhood; you will care nothing for the beauties that used to take your breath away and kindle such a longing in you, and many others like you, Socrates, to be always at the side of the beloved and feasting your eyes upon him, so that you would be content, if it were possible, to deny yourself the grosser necessities of meat and drink, so long as you were with him.

"But if it were given to man to gaze on beauty's very self—unsullied, unalloyed, and freed from the mortal taint that haunts the frailer loveliness of flesh and blood—if, I say, it were given to man to see the heavenly beauty face to face, would you call *his*," she asked me, "an unenviable life, whose eyes had been opened to the vision, and who had gazed upon it in true contemplation until it had become his own forever?

"And remember," she said, "that it is only when he discerns beauty itself through what makes it visible that a man will be quickened with the true, and not the seeming virtue—for it is virtue's self that quickens him, not virtue's semblance. And when he has brought forth and reared this perfect virtue, he shall be called the friend of God, and if ever it is given to man to put on immortality, it shall be given to him."

Translated by Michael Joyce

Phaedrus: But let us go, now that it has become less oppressively hot.

Socrates: Shouldn't we first offer a prayer?

Phaedrus: Of course.

Socrates: Dear Pan, and all you other gods who live here, grant that I may become beautiful within, and that whatever outward things I have may be in harmony with the spirit inside me. May I understand that it is only the wise who are rich, and may I have only as much money as a temperate person needs. —Is there anything else that we can ask for, Phaedrus? For me, that prayer is enough.

Phaedrus: Make it a prayer for me too, since friends have all things in common.

Socrates: Let's be going.

CHUANG-TZU (369?–286? B.C.E.)

All descriptions of the Tao are metaphors, ways of pointing to the reality beyond words. These old boys Lao-tzu and Chuang-tzu sound paradoxical because they are always trying to include the two opposite and complementary aspects of a truth, which logic wants us to choose between. Must we choose between left eye and right eye?

If Lao-tzu's humor is like a smile, Chuang-tzu's is like a raucous belly-laugh. He is the clown of the Absolute, the apotheosis of incredulity, Coyote among the Bodhisattvas. Is he a little crazy? Or are you not crazy enough? He tilts like the great earth itself, spinning in empty space.

Everything has its "that," everything has its "this." From the point of view of "that" you cannot see it, but through understanding you can know it. So I say, "that" comes out of "this" and "this" depends on "that"—which is to say that "this" and "that" give birth to each other. But where there is birth there must be death; where there is death there must be birth. Where there is acceptability there must be unacceptability; where there is unacceptability there must be acceptability. Where there is recognition of right there must be recognition of wrong; where there is recognition of wrong there must be recognition of right. Therefore the sage does not proceed in such a way, but illuminates all in the light of Heaven. He too recognizes a "this," but a "this" which is also "that," a "that" which is also "this." His "that" has both a right and a wrong in it. So, in fact, does he still have a "this" and "that"? Or does he in fact no longer have a "this" and "that"? A state in which "this" and "that" no longer find their opposites is called the hinge of the Way. When the hinge is fitted into the socket, it can respond endlessly. Its right then is a single endlessness and its wrong too is a single endlessness. So, I say, the best thing to use is clarity.

To use an attribute to show that attributes are not attributes is

18

not as good a thing as using a nonattribute to show that attributes are not attributes. To use a horse to show that a horse is not a horse is not as good as using a non-horse to show that a horse is not a horse. Heaven and earth are one attribute; the ten thousand things are one horse.

What is acceptable we call acceptable; what is unacceptable we call unacceptable. A road is made by people walking on it; things are so because they are called so. What makes them so? Making them so makes them so. What makes them not so? Making them not so makes them not so. Things all must have that which is so; things all must have that which is acceptable. There is nothing that is not so, nothing that is not acceptable.

For this reason, whether you point to a little stalk or a great pillar, a leper or the beautiful Hsi-shih, things ribald and shady or things grotesque and strange, the Way makes them all into one. Their dividedness is their completeness; their completeness is their impairment. No thing is either complete or impaired, but all are made into one again. Only the man of far-reaching vision knows how to make them into one. So he has no use for categories, but relegates all to the constant. The constant is the useful; the useful is the passable; the passable is the successful; and with success, all is accomplished. He relies upon this alone, relies upon it and does not know he is doing so. This is called the Way.

But to wear out your brain trying to make things into one without realizing that they are all the same—this is called "three in the morning." What do I mean by "three in the morning"? When the monkey trainer was handing out acorns, he said, "You get three in the morning and four at night." This made all the monkeys furious. "Well, then," he said, "you get four in the morning and three at night." The monkeys were all delighted. There was no change in the reality behind the words, and yet the monkeys responded with joy and anger. Let them, if they want to. So the sage harmonizes with both right and wrong and rests in Heaven the Equalizer.

Now I am going to make a statement here. I don't know whether it fits into the category of other people's statements or not. But whether it fits into their category or whether it doesn't, it obviously fits into some category. So in that respect it is no different from their statements. However, let me try making my statement.

There is a beginning. There is a not yet beginning to be a beginning. There is a not yet beginning to be a not yet beginning to be a beginning. There is being. There is nonbeing. There is a not yet beginning to be nonbeing. There is a not yet beginning to be a not yet beginning to be nonbeing. Suddenly there is nonbeing. But I do not know, when it comes to nonbeing, which is really being and which is nonbeing. Now I have just said something. But I don't know whether what I have said has really said something or whether it hasn't said something.

There is nothing in the world bigger than the tip of an autumn hair, and Mount T'ai is tiny. No one has lived longer than a dead child, and P'eng-tsu died young. Heaven and earth were born at the same time as I was, and the ten thousand things are one with me.

We have already become one, so how can I say anything? But I have just *said* that we are one, so how can I not be saying something? The one and what I said about it make two, and two and the original one make three. If we go on this way, then even the cleverest mathematician can't tell where we'll end, much less an ordinary man. If by moving from nonbeing to being we get to three, how far will we get if we move from being to being? Better not to move, but to let things be!

The Way has never known boundaries; speech has no constancy. But because of the recognition of a "this," there came to be boundaries. Let me tell you what the boundaries are. There is left, there is right, there are theories, there are debates, there are discriminations, there are emulations, and there are contentions. These are called the Eight Virtues. As to what is beyond the Six Realms, the sage admits its existence but does not theorize. As to what is within the Six Realms, he theorizes but does not debate. In the case of the *Spring and Autumn*, the record of the former kings of past ages, the sage debates but does not discriminate. So I say, those who divide fail to divide; those who discriminate fail to discriminate. What does this mean, you ask? The sage embraces things. Ordinary men discriminate among them and parade their discriminations before others. So I say, those who discriminate fail to see.

The Great Way is not named; Great Discriminations are not spoken; Great Benevolence is not benevolent; Great Modesty is not humble; Great Daring does not attack. If the Way is made clear, it is not the Way. If discriminations are put into words, they do not suffice. If benevolence has a constant object, it cannot be universal. If modesty is fastidious, it cannot be trusted. If daring attacks, it cannot be complete. These five are all round, but they tend toward the square.

Therefore understanding that rests in what it does not understand is the finest. Who can understand discriminations that are not spoken, the Way that is not a way? If he can understand this, he may be called the Reservoir of Heaven. Pour into it and it is never full, dip from it and it never runs dry, and yet it does not know where the supply comes from. This is called the Shaded Light.

———

Chu Ch'ueh-tzu said to Chang Wu-tzu, "I have heard Confucius say that the sage does not work at anything, does not pursue profit, does not dodge harm, does not enjoy being sought after, does not follow the Way, says nothing yet says something, says something yet says nothing, and wanders beyond the dust and grime. Confucius himself regarded these as wild and flippant words, though I believe they describe the working of the mysterious Way. What do you think of them?"

Chang Wu-tzu said, "Even the Yellow Emperor would be confused if he heard such words, so how could you expect Confucius to understand them? What's more, you're too hasty in your own appraisal. You see an egg and demand a crowing cock, see a crossbow and demand a roast dove. I'm going to try speaking some reckless words and I want you to listen to them recklessly. How will that be? The sage leans on the sun and moon, tucks the universe under his arm, merges himself with things, leaves the confusion and muddle as it is, and looks on slaves as exalted. Ordinary men strain and struggle; the sage is stupid and blockish. He takes part in ten thousand ages and achieves simplicity in oneness. For him, all the ten thousand things are what they are, and thus they enfold each other.

"How do I know that loving life is not a delusion? How do I know that in hating death I am not like a man who, having left home in his youth, has forgotten the way back?

"Lady Li was the daughter of the border guard of Ai. When she was first taken captive and brought to the state of Chin, she wept until her tears drenched the collar of her robe. But later, when she went to live in the palace of the ruler, shared his couch with him, and ate the delicious meats of his table, she wondered why she had ever wept. How do I know that the dead do not wonder why they ever longed for life?

"He who dreams of drinking wine may weep when morning comes; he who dreams of weeping may in the morning go off to hunt. While he is dreaming he does not know it is a dream, and in his dream he may even try to interpret a dream. Only after he wakes does he know it was a dream. And someday there will be a great awakening when we know that this is all a great dream. Yet the stupid believe they are awake, busily and brightly assuming they understand things, calling this man ruler, that one herdsman—how dense! Confucius and you are both dreaming! And when I say you are dreaming, I am dreaming too. Words like these will be labeled the Supreme Swindle."

The True Man of ancient times did not rebel against want, did not grow proud in plenty, and did not plan his affairs. A man like this could commit an error and not regret it, could meet with success and not make a show. A man like this could climb the high places and not be frightened, could enter the water and not get wet, could enter the fire and not get burned. His knowledge was able to climb all the way up to the Way like this.

The True Man of ancient times slept without dreaming and woke without care; he ate without savoring and his breath came from deep inside. The True Man breathes with his heels; the mass of men breathe with their throats. Crushed and bound down, they gasp out their words as though they were retching. Deep in their passions and desires, they are shallow in the workings of heaven.

The True Man of ancient times knew nothing of loving life, knew nothing of hating death. He emerged without delight; he went back in without a fuss. He came briskly, he went briskly, and that was all. He didn't forget where he began; he didn't try to find out where he would end. He received something and took pleasure in it; he forgot about it and handed it back again.

Translated by Burton Watson

The traditional Jewish (and Christian) sage is a solemn fellow, like the traditional Jewish (and Christian) God. Philo knows better.

God loves to give, and freely bestows good things on all people, even the imperfect, inviting them to participate in virtue and to love it, and at the same time manifesting his superabundant wealth, which is more than enough for as many as wish to profit from it. He shows this in nature as well. For when he sends rain on the ocean, and causes springs to gush in the most desolate wastelands, and makes sterile soil blossom with grass and flowers, what is he showing but the extravagance of his wealth and goodness? That is why every soul he created has the seed of goodness in it.

———

"Today" means boundless and inexhaustible eternity. Periods of months and years and of time in general are ideas of men, who calculate by number; but the true name of eternity is Today.

———

God alone, in the precise sense of the word, celebrates holidays. He alone rejoices, he alone feels delight, he alone is happy, he alone enjoys absolute peace; he has no grief or fear, is free of any evil or pain, and lives in eternal bliss. His nature is absolutely perfect, or rather, God is the height, the goal, and the limit of happiness. There is nothing outside himself that he needs, but he has given a share of his own beauty to all particular beings, from the fountain of beauty: himself. For all the beautiful things in the world would never have been what they are if they hadn't been modeled after the archetype of true beauty, the Uncreated, the Blessed, the Imperishable.

———

The face of the wise man is not somber or austere, contracted by anxiety and sorrow, but precisely the opposite: radiant and serene, and filled with a vast delight, which often makes him the most playful of men, acting with a sense of humor that blends with his essential seriousness and dignity, just as in a well-tuned lyre all the notes blend into one harmonious sound. According to our holy teacher Moses, the goal of wisdom is laughter and play—not the kind that one sees in little children who do not yet have the faculty of reason, but the kind that is developed in those who have grown mature through both time and understanding. If someone has experienced the wisdom that can only be heard from oneself, learned from oneself, and created from oneself, he does not merely participate in laughter: he becomes laughter itself.

—————

When the righteous man searches for the nature of all things, he makes his own admirable discovery: that everything is God's grace. Every being in the world, and the world itself, manifests the blessings and generosity of God.

These simple, luminous words come from the depths of the human heart.

Love your enemies, do good to those who hate you, bless those who curse you, and pray for those who mistreat you, so that you may be children of your Father in heaven: for he makes his sun rise on the evil and on the good, and sends rain to the just and to the unjust.

———

Don't be anxious about what you will eat or what you will wear. Isn't your life more than its food, and your body more than its clothing? Look at the birds of the sky: they neither sow nor reap nor gather into barns, yet God feeds them. Which of you by thinking can add a day to his life? And why do you worry about clothing? Consider the lilies of the field, how they grow: they neither toil nor spin. And yet I tell you that not even Solomon in all his glory was robed like one of these. Therefore, if God so clothes the grass, which grows in the field today, and tomorrow is thrown into the oven, won't he all the more clothe you? So don't worry about these things and say, "What will we eat?" or "What will we wear?" For this is what worldly people seek; and your Father knows that you need these things. But first seek the kingdom of God; and these things will be given to you as well.

———

Ask, and it will be given to you; seek, and you will find; knock, and the door will be opened to you. For everyone who asks, receives; and he who seeks, finds; and to him who knocks, the door will be opened.

———

Don't judge, and you will not be judged; don't condemn, and you will not be condemned; forgive, and you will be forgiven; give, and it will be given to you: they will pour into your lap good measure, pressed down, shaken together, and overflowing. For the measure by which you give is the measure by which you will receive.

———

Unless you change your life and become like a child, you cannot enter the kingdom of heaven.

———

There once was a man who had two sons. And the younger one said to him, "Father, let me have my share of the estate." So he divided his property between them. And not many days afterward, having turned his share into money, the younger son left and traveled to a distant country, and there he squandered his inheritance in riotous living. And after he had spent it all, a severe famine arose in that country; and he was destitute. And he went and hired himself out to a citizen of that country, who sent him to his farm to feed the pigs. And he longed to fill his belly with the husks that the pigs were eating; and no one would give him any food. And when he came to himself, he said, "How many of my father's hired men have more than enough to eat, while I am dying of hunger. I will get up and go to my father, and say to him, 'Father, I have sinned against God and against you, and I am no longer worthy to be called your son. Let me be like one of your hired men.'" And he got up, and went to his father. And while he was still a long way off, his father saw him, and was moved with compassion, and ran to him, and threw his arms around him, and kissed him. And the son said to him, "Father, I have sinned against God and against you, and I am no longer worthy to be called your son." But the father said to his servants, "Quick, bring out the best robe we have and put it on him; and put a ring on his hand, and sandals on his feet. And bring the fatted calf, and kill it; and let us eat and make merry. For this son of mine was dead, and he has come back to life; he was lost, and is found." And they began to make merry.

Now the older son had been out in the fields; and on his way home, as he got closer to the house, he heard music and dancing, and he called over one of the servants and asked what was happening. And the servant said, "Your brother has come, and your father has killed the fatted calf, because he has him back safe and sound." And he was angry and would not go in. And his father came out and tried to soothe him; but he said, "Look: all these years I have been serving you, and never have I disobeyed your command. Yet you never even gave me a goat, so that I could feast and make merry with my friends. But now that this son of yours comes back, after eating up your money on whores, you kill the fatted calf for him!" And the father said to him, "Child, you are always with me, and everything I have is yours. But it was proper to make merry and rejoice, for your brother was dead, and he has come back to life; he was lost, and is found."

———

The kingdom of God does not come if you watch for it. Nor will anyone be able to say, "It is here" or "It is there." For the kingdom of God is within you.

———◎———

Look around. Read the headlines. How can the kingdom of heaven already be here?

When we change the way we see the world, we change the world.

Jesus said, "If your teachers say to you, 'Look, the kingdom is in heaven,' then the birds will get there before you. But the kingdom is inside you, and it is outside you. If you know yourselves, then you will be known; and you will know that you are the sons of the living Father."

———

Jesus said, "Recognize what is in your sight, and what is hidden will become clear to you."

———

Jesus said, "When you see one who was not born of a woman, bow down and worship him. That one is your Father."

———

The disciples said to him, "Tell us what our end will be." Jesus said, "If you haven't found the beginning, why ask about the end? For where the beginning is, the end is also. Blessed are those who stand at the beginning, for they will know the end, and they will not taste death."

———

Jesus saw some infants nursing. He said to his disciples, "These infants are like those who enter the kingdom of heaven." They said to him, "How then can we enter?" Jesus said to them, "When you make the two one, and when you make the inside like the outside, and the outside like the inside, and the upper like the lower, and when you make male and female into a single one, then you will enter the kingdom."

———

Jesus said, "Blessed are those who have chosen their solitude, for they will find the kingdom of heaven."

———

The disciples said to him, "When will the repose of the dead happen, and when will the new world come?" Jesus said, "What you are waiting for has already come, but you don't recognize it."

———

Jesus said, "Whoever believes that the All is deficient is himself deficient."

———

Jesus said, "If you bring forth what is inside you, what you bring forth will save you. If you don't bring forth what is inside you, what you don't bring forth will destroy you."

———

Jesus said, "I am the light that shines over everything. I am the All. From me the All came forth, and to me the All has returned. Split a piece of wood, and I am there. Pick up a stone, and you will find me there."

———

The disciples said to him, "Tell us who you are, so that we can trust you." Jesus said, "You search for me through heaven and earth, but you don't know the one who is right before your eyes, because you don't know how to search into this very moment."

———

The disciples said to him, "When will the kingdom come?" Jesus said, "It will not come if you look for it. Nor can you say, 'It is here' or 'It is there.' For the kingdom of the Father is already spread out over the earth, but people don't see it."

Logos ("Word") can also be translated as "the Primal Harmony" or "the Tao." Whenever we are true to ourselves, the Word becomes flesh and dwells among us.

In the beginning was the Word, and the Word was with God, and the Word was God.

———

To all who receive him, he gives the power to become children of God.

———

You will know the truth, and the truth will make you free.

———

The spirit you have received from him remains in you, and you don't need to have any man teach you; but that spirit teaches you all things, and is the truth.

———

Love comes from God, and everyone who loves is begotten by God and knows God; those who don't love, don't know God; for God is love.

———

"Behold, I make all things new. I am alpha and omega, the beginning and the end."

Jewish, Christian, and Moslem cultures, seeing the First Commandment from the outside, have traditionally been ignorant and cruel toward pagan practices. Though he doesn't see to the center, Maximus sees with the heart. May his lovely tolerance be an example for us all.

God himself, the father and fashioner of all that is, older than the sun or the sky, greater than time and eternity and all the flow of being, is unnamable by any lawgiver, unutterable by any voice, not to be seen by any eye. But we, being unable to apprehend his essence, use the help of sounds and names and pictures, of beaten gold and ivory and silver, of plants and rivers, mountain peaks and torrents, yearning for the knowledge of him, and in our weakness naming all that is beautiful in this world after his nature—just as happens to earthly lovers. To them the most beautiful sight will be the actual lineaments of the beloved. But for remembrance' sake they will be happy in the sight of a lyre, a little spear, a chair perhaps, or a running ground, or anything in the world that awakens the memory of the beloved. Why should I further examine and pass judgment about images? Let men know what is divine. Let them know. That is all. If a Greek is stirred to the remembrance of God by the art of Phidias, an Egyptian by paying worship to animals, another man by a river, another by fire, I have no anger for their divergences. Only let them know, let them love, let them remember.

Translator unknown

Becoming everything is just another method of becoming nothing. If you go far enough east, you'll arrive at the west.

But be careful. The person who says "I am God" may be a raving ego-maniac. If you are everything, or even if you are anything, why say it? Isn't it better to sit in the back yard, watching God with God's eyes?

If you don't make yourself equal to God, you can't perceive God; for like is known by like. Leap free of everything that is physical, and grow as vast as that immeasurable vastness; step beyond all time and become eternal; then you will perceive God. Realize that nothing is impossible for you; recognize that you too are immortal and that you can embrace all things in your mind; find your home in the heart of every living creature; make yourself higher than all heights and lower than all depths; bring all opposites inside yourself and reconcile them; understand that you are everywhere, on the land, in the sea, in the sky; realize that you haven't yet been begotten, that you are still in the womb, that you are young, that you are old, that you are dead, that you are in the world beyond the grave; hold all this in your mind, all times and places, all substances and qualities and magnitudes; then you can perceive God.

Wanting to know God is the road that leads to God, and it is an easy road to travel. God will come to meet you everywhere, he will appear to you everywhere, at times and places when you don't expect it, while you are awake and while you are asleep, while you are traveling and while you are at home, while you are speaking and while you are silent; for there is nothing in which God does not exist. And don't think that God is invisible. Who is more evident than God? That is why he made all things, so that through all things you can see him.

Vajrachedika is more accurately translated as "the Diamond Cutter": a scripture of such highly compressed, adamantine wisdom that it can cut through doubt as a diamond cuts through glass.

Any Bodhisattva who undertakes the practice of meditation should cherish one thought only: "When I attain perfect wisdom, I will liberate all sentient beings in every realm of the universe, and allow them to pass into the eternal peace of Nirvana." And yet, when vast, uncountable, unthinkable myriads of beings have been liberated, truly no being has been liberated. Why? Because no Bodhisattva who is a true Bodhisattva entertains such concepts as "self" or "others." Thus there are no sentient beings to be liberated and no self to attain perfect wisdom.

———

The Buddha has no doctrine to convey. The truth is ungraspable and inexpressible. It neither is nor is not.

———

All Bodhisattvas should develop a pure, lucid mind that doesn't depend upon sight, sound, touch, flavor, smell, or any thought that arises in it. A Bodhisattva should develop a mind that alights nowhere.

———

The mind should be kept independent of any thoughts that arise within it. If the mind depends upon anything, it has no sure haven.

———

When I attained Absolute Perfect Enlightenment, I attained absolutely nothing. That is why it is called Absolute Perfect Enlightenment.

The nineteenth-century Hasidic rabbi Menahem Mendel of Kotzk once asked some visiting scholars, "Where does God dwell?" They laughed at him and said, "God is everywhere, of course. 'The whole earth is full of his glory.'" The rabbi shook his head, then said, "God dwells wherever man lets him in."

The divine nature, as it is in itself, according to its essence, transcends every act of comprehensive knowledge, and it cannot be approached or attained by our speculation. Men have never discovered a faculty to comprehend the incomprehensible; nor have we ever been able to devise an intellectual technique for grasping the inconceivable. For this reason the apostle Paul calls God's ways "unsearchable," teaching us by this that the way which leads to the knowledge of the divine nature is inaccessible to our reason; and hence none of those who have lived before us has given us the slightest hint of comprehension suggesting that we might know that which in itself is above all knowledge.

Such then is he whose essence is above every nature, invisible, incomprehensible. Yet he can be seen and apprehended in another way, and the ways of this apprehension are numerous. For we can see him, who has "made all things in wisdom," by the process of inference through the wisdom that is reflected in the universe. It is just as in human works of art, where the mind can in a sense see the author of the ordered structure that is before it, inasmuch as he has left his artistry in his work. But notice that what we see here is not the substance of the craftsman, but merely the artistic skill that he has impressed in his work. So too, when we consider the order of creation, we form an image not of the substance but of the wisdom of him who has made all things wisely. Again, when we consider the origin of human life, how God came to create man not out of any necessity but merely by the goodness of his free will, we say that we again contemplate God in this way, but it is his goodness and not his essence that is the object of our knowledge. So it is with all the things that raise the mind toward the supreme good; in all these cases we may speak of a knowledge of God, since all these sublime considerations bring God within our ken. For the concepts of power, purity, immutability, freedom from limitation by what is contrary, and the like, impress upon our minds the image of a sublime and, in a sense, divine idea.

From what has been said, then, it is clear that the Lord does not deceive us when he promises that the pure in heart "shall see God"; nor does Paul deceive us when he teaches us in his epistles that no one has seen God nor can see him. For being by nature invisible, he becomes visible only in his operations, and only when he is contemplated in the things that are external to him.

But the meaning of this Beatitude does not merely indicate that we can infer the nature of the cause from its operations; for in that case even the wise of this world might gain a knowledge of transcendent wisdom and power through the harmonic structure of the universe. Rather, I think that this magnificent Beatitude envisages another counsel for those who are able to receive and grasp what they desire. My meaning will become clear by examples.

In our human existence physical health is a good thing; and indeed it is a blessing not only to know the reasons for good health but actually to enjoy it. Now suppose a man should speak the praises of good health and then proceed to take food that was unwholesome and contained unhealthy juices. What good would his praise of health be, when he himself was afflicted with disease?

Analogously, then, we are to penetrate the meaning of our present text. The Lord does not say that it is blessed to know something about God, but rather to possess God in oneself: "Blessed are the clean of heart, for they shall see God." By this I do not think he means that the man who purifies the eye of his soul will enjoy an immediate vision of God; rather I think this marvelous saying teaches us the same lesson that the Word expressed more clearly to others when he said: "The kingdom of God is within you." And this teaches us that the man who purifies his heart of every creature and of every destructive passion will see the image of the divine nature in his own beauty. So too in this short sentence the Word, I think, is giving us the following advice: All you mortals who have within yourselves a desire to behold the supreme good, when you are told that the majesty of God is exalted above the heavens, that the divine glory is inexpressible, its beauty indescribable, its nature inaccessible, do not despair at never being able to behold what you desire. For you do have within your grasp the degree of the knowledge of God which you can attain. For when God made you, he at once endowed your nature with this perfection: upon the structure of your nature he imprinted an imitation of the perfections of his own nature, just as one would impress upon wax the outline of an emblem. But the wickedness that has been poured all over this divine engraving has made your perfection useless and hidden it with a vicious coating. You must then wash away, by a life of virtue, the dirt that has come to cling to your heart like plaster, and then your divine beauty will once again shine forth.

The same thing happens with iron. Though it might once have been black, as soon as it has been cleaned of rust with a whetstone it begins to shine and glisten and give off rays in the sun. So it is with the interior man (for that is what our Lord refers to by the word "heart"). Once he has scraped off the rustlike dirt that has accumulated on his form because of evil degeneration, then he will become good once more and shine forth in the likeness of his archetype. For surely what resembles the good is in itself good. Thus, if such a man will look at himself, he will see within himself the object of his desire; and thus he will become "blessed," for in gazing upon his own purity he will see the archetype within the image.

It is just like men who look at the sun in a mirror. Even though they do not look up directly at the heavens, they see the sun in the mirror's reflection just as much as those who look directly at the sun. So it is, says our Lord, with you. Even though you are not strong enough to see the light itself, yet you will find within yourselves what you are seeking, if you would only return to the grace of that image which was established within you from the beginning. For the Godhead is all purity, freedom from passion, the absence of all evil. And if you possess these qualities, God will surely be within you. When your mind is untainted by any evil, free of passion, purified of all stain, then you will be "blessed" because your eye is clear. Then, because you have been purified, you will perceive things that are invisible to the unpurified. The dark cloud of matter will be removed from the eye of your soul, and then you will see clearly that blessed vision within the pure brilliance of your own heart. And what is this vision? It is purity, holiness, simplicity, and other such brilliant reflections of the nature of God; for it is in these that God is seen.

Translated by Herbert Musurillo, S. J.

It is water and fire, darkness and light, father and mother, everything, nothing. How can we trust it with our whole heart? One plus one equals one.

There is a love like a small lamp, which goes out when the oil is consumed; or like a stream, which dries up when it doesn't rain. But there is a love that is like a mighty spring gushing up out of the earth; it keeps flowing forever, and is inexhaustible.

———

When we trust God with our whole heart, we don't fill our prayers with "Give me this" or "Take this from me." We don't even think of ourselves when we pray. At every moment we trust our Father in heaven, whose love infinitely surpasses the love of all earthly fathers and who gives us more than we ourselves could ask for or even imagine.

———

Humility collects the soul into a single point by the power of silence. A truly humble man has no desire to be known or admired by others, but wishes to plunge from himself into himself, to become nothing, as if he had never been born. When he is completely hidden to himself in himself, he is completely with God.

The Net of Indra is a profound and subtle metaphor for the structure of reality. Imagine a vast net; at each crossing point there is a jewel; each jewel is perfectly clear and reflects all the other jewels in the net, the way two mirrors placed opposite each other will reflect an image ad infinitum. The jewel in this metaphor stands for an individual being, or an individual consciousness, or a cell, or an atom. Every jewel is intimately connected with all other jewels in the universe, and a change in one jewel means a change, however slight, in every other jewel. Thus, by liberating yourself, you liberate all beings in the universe. Or, from the opposite direction: Once, when someone praised Gandhi for his compassionate politics, he answered, "I am here to serve no one else but myself, to find my own self-realization through the service of others."

Knowledge accords with things, being in one and the same realm, made by conditions, tacitly conjoining, without rejecting anything, suddenly appearing, yet not without before and after. Therefore scripture says, "The sphere of the universal eye, the pure body, I now will expound; let people listen carefully." By way of explanation, the "universal eye" is the union of knowledge and reality, all at once revealing many things. This makes it clear that reality is known to the knowledge of the universal eye only and is not the sphere of any other knowledge. The "sphere" means things. This illustrates how the many things interpenetrate like the realm of Indra's net of jewels—multiplied and remultiplied ad infinitum. The pure body illustrates how all things, as mentioned before, simultaneously enter one another. Ends and beginnings, being collectively formed by conditional origination, are impossible to trace to a basis—the seeing mind has nothing to rest on.

Now the celestial jewel net of Kanishka, or Indra, Emperor of Gods, is called the net of Indra. This imperial net is made all of jewels: because the jewels are clear, they reflect one another's images, appearing in one another's reflections upon reflections, ad infinitum, all appearing at once in one jewel, and in each one it is so—ultimately there is no going or coming.

Now for a moment let us turn to the southwest direction and pick a jewel and examine it. This jewel can show the reflections of all the jewels at once—and just as this is so of this jewel, so it is of every other jewel: the reflection is multiplied and remultiplied over and over endlessly. These infinitely multiplying jewel reflections are all in one jewel and show clearly—the others do not hinder this. If you sit in one jewel, then you are sitting in all the jewels in every direction, multiplied over and over. Why? Because in one jewel there are all the jewels. If there is one jewel in all the jewels, then you are sitting in all the jewels too. And the reverse applies to the totality, if you follow the same reasoning. Since in one jewel you go into all the jewels without leaving this one jewel, so in all jewels you enter one jewel without leaving this one jewel.

Question: If you say that one enters all the jewels in one jewel without ever leaving this one jewel, how is it possible to enter all the jewels?

Answer: It is precisely by not leaving this one jewel that you can enter all the jewels. If you left this one jewel to enter all the jewels, you couldn't enter all the jewels. Why? Because outside this jewel there are no separate jewels.

Question: If there are no jewels outside this one jewel, then this net is made of one jewel. How can you say then that it's made of many jewels tied together?

Answer: It is precisely because there is one jewel that many can be joined to form a net. Why? Because this one jewel alone forms the net—that is, if you take away this jewel there will be no net.

Question: If there is only one jewel, how can you speak of tying it into a net?

Answer: Tying many jewels to form a net is itself just one jewel.

Why? "One" is the aspect of totality, containing the many in its formation. Since all would not exist if there were not one, this net is therefore made by one jewel. The all entering the one can be known by thinking about it in this way.

Question: Although the jewel in the southwest contains all the jewels in the ten directions completely, without remainder, there are jewels in every direction. How can you say then that the net is made of just one jewel?

Answer: All the jewels in the ten directions are in totality the one jewel of the southwest. Why? The jewel in the southwest *is* all the jewels of the ten directions. If you don't believe that one jewel in the southwest is all the jewels of the ten directions, just put a dot on the jewel in the southwest. When one jewel is dotted, there are dots on all the jewels in all directions. Since there are dots on all the jewels in all directions, we know that all the jewels are one jewel. If anyone says that all the jewels in the ten directions are not one jewel in the southwest, could it be that one person simultaneously put dots on all the jewels in the ten directions? Even allowing the universal dotting of all the jewels in the ten directions, they are just one jewel. Since it is thus, using this one as beginning, the same is so when taking others first—multiplied over and over boundlessly, each dot is the same. It is obscure and hard to fathom: when one is complete, all is done. Such a subtle metaphor is applied to things to help us think about them, but things are not so; a simile is the same as not a simile—they resemble each other in a way, so we use it to speak of. What does this mean? These jewels only have their reflected images containing and entering one another—their substances are separate. Things are not like this, because their whole substance merges completely. The book on natural origination in the Flower Garland scripture says, "In order to benefit sentient beings and make them all understand, nonsimiles are used to illustrate real truth. Such a subtle teaching as this is hard to hear even in

43

immeasurable eons; only those with perseverance and wisdom can hear of the matrix of the issue of thusness." The scripture says, "Nonsimiles are used as similes. Those who practice should think of this in accord with the similes."

Translated by Thomas Cleary

Islam means "surrender to God." When we surrender ourselves fully, there is nothing but God: not even a "there"; not even an "is"; not even a "God."

"Have they not beheld the heaven above them, how We established and adorned it in its unbroken reach? And the earth also We stretched out, setting on it the mighty hills, where We made every kind of joyous thing to grow for insight and for token to every penitent servant. From heaven We have sent down the blessed rain by which We make the gardens grow, and grain of harvest and tall palm trees laden with clustered dates, in provision for men, thereby bringing again to life a land that was dead—similitude of the coming forth.

"We created man: We know the very whisperings within him and We are closer to him than his jugular vein."

———

All that is in the heavens and in the earth magnifies God. He is the all-strong, the all-wise. To Him belongs the kingdom of the heavens and of the earth. He gives life and He brings on death and He is omnipotent over all things. He is the first and the last, the manifest and the hidden, and has knowledge of all things. It is He who created the heavens and the earth in six days and then assumed His Throne. He knows all that permeates the ground and all that issues from it, what comes down from the heaven and what ascends into it. He is with you wherever you are. He is aware of all you do.

His is the kingdom of the heavens and of the earth and to Him all things return. He makes the night to give way to the day and the day to the night, and He knows the innermost heart.

Translated by Kenneth Cragg

———

Do not despise the world, for the world too is God.

———

Wherever you turn is God's face.

———

"My servant does not cease to come near Me until I love him; and when I love him, I am the sight he sees with and the hearing he hears with and the hand he receives with and the foot he walks with."

———

Whoever knows himself knows God.

———

True religion is surrender.

———◦———

When we consider absolute reality, there is no end, no beginning; emptiness is the same as fullness, just seen from a different perspective. We say
that this coffee cup is empty; but empty means filled with space, filled with
possibilities, ready for anything: milk, water, tea, wine. Every moment of
time, every point in space, is completely empty, completely open for what
wants to come. That is why it can be filled. ("Behold, I make all things
new.")

The following passage is a commentary (eleven hundred years before
the fact) on William Blake's famous quatrain:

> To see a World in a Grain of Sand
> And a Heaven in a Wild Flower,
> Hold Infinity in the palm of your hand
> And Eternity in an hour.

As for the three universals, first is the universal of one atom pervad-
ing the universe: this means that an atom has no inherent nature—
it involves all reality in its establishment. Since reality is boundless,
so accordingly is the atom. The scripture says, "In all the atoms in
the Flower Treasury world, in each atom the universe is seen; jewel
lights show Buddhas like clouds gathering. This is the freedom in all
fields of the enlightened." According to this teaching, it should be
known that one atom pervades the universe.

Second is the universal of one atom producing infinity. This
means that the atom has no essence of its own and its becoming
must depend on reality. Since true thusness contains innumerable
qualities, the functions arising from reality also have myriad differ-
ences. The "Treatise on Awakening of Faith" says, "Real thusness
has of its own essence the meaning of eternity, bliss, self, and purity,
the meaning of pure, cool, unchanging freedom; it contains innumerable such qualities, so ultimately it has not the slightest lack."

Therefore the Flower Garland scripture says, "In this Flower Treasury ocean of worlds, whether it be mountains or rivers, down to trees, forests, even a mote of dust, a hair—not one is not in accord with the universe of true thusness, including boundless qualities." By this teaching it should be known that an atom is at once noumenon and phenomenon, is person and is thing, is "that" and is "this," is object and is subject, is defiled and is pure, is cause and is effect, is same and is different, is one and is many, is broad and is narrow, is animate and is inanimate, is the three bodies and is the ten bodies.

Why? Since phenomena and noumenon are without interference, phenomenon and phenomenon are without mutual interference. Because things are like this, the ten bodies together perform free functioning; therefore it is only within the purview of enlightening beings with the universal eye. Among the phenomenal characteristics cited, each one again contains the others, includes the others—each contains infinitely multiplied and remultiplied delineations of objects. The scripture says, "The inexhaustible ocean of all teachings is converged on the enlightenment site of a single thing. The nature of things as such is explained by the Buddha: the eye of wisdom can understand this technique."

Question: According to this explanation, then, in a single atom no principle is not revealed, no phenomenon is not merged, no passage is not explained, no meaning is not conveyed. How can those not cultivating and studying in the present become enlightened at an atom and settle manifold doubts all at once? And in the atom, what is called defilement, what is called purity? What is called real, what is called conventional? What is called birth-and-death, what is called nirvana? What is called the principle of the lesser vehicle, what is called the principle of the greater vehicle? Please give us some definitions and let us hear what we have not yet heard.

Answer: Great knowledge, round and clear, looks at a fine hair and comprehends the ocean of nature; the source of reality is clearly manifest in one atom, yet illumines the whole of being. When myriad phenomena arise, they must be at the same time, in one space—noumenon has no before or after. Why? Because the illusory characteristics of this atom can block the vision of reality, it is defiled; because this atom's characteristics are empty and nonexistent, it is pure. Because this atom's fundamental essence is the same as thusness, it is real; because its characteristics are conditionally produced and exist as illusions, it is artificial. Because thoughts of the atom's characteristics change every moment, it is birth-and-death; because, when we observe the atom in contemplation, the signs of origination and annihilation of the atom's characteristics are all empty and without reality, it is nirvana. Because the atom's characteristics, great or small, are all discriminations of the deluded mind, it is affliction; because the essence of the atom's characteristics is without mental construction, it is the principle of the lesser vehicle; because the nature of the atom has no birth, no destruction, and depends on others for its seeming existence, it is the principle of the greater vehicle.

In this way I explain in brief; if it were said in full, even if all sentient beings had doubts, each different, and questioned the Buddha, the Buddha would simply use the one word "atom" to solve and explain for them. This should be pondered deeply. The scripture says, "The inexhaustible ocean of all truths is expounded in a single word, completely, without remainder." Based on this teaching it is called the universal of one atom producing infinity.

Third is the universal of an atom containing emptiness and existence. This means that the atom has no intrinsic nature, so it is empty; yet its illusory characteristics are evident, so it is existent. Indeed, because illusory form has no essence, it must be no different from emptiness, and real emptiness contains qualities permeating to the surface of existence. Seeing that form is empty produces great wisdom and not dwelling in birth-and-death; seeing that emptiness is form produces great compassion and not dwelling in nirvana. When form and emptiness are nondual, compassion and wisdom are not different; only this is true seeing.

The *Ratnagotra-shastra* says, "Bodhisattvas before the Path still have three doubts about this real emptiness and inconceivable existence. The first is that they suspect that emptiness annihilates form and hence grasp nihilistic emptiness. The second is that they suspect that emptiness is different from form and hence grasp emptiness outside of form. The third is that they suspect that emptiness is a thing and hence grasp emptiness as an entity."

Now I must explain this. Form is illusory form and necessarily does not interfere with emptiness. Emptiness is true emptiness and necessarily does not interfere with form. If it interfered with form, it would be nihilistic emptiness. If it interfered with emptiness, it would be solid form. Since one atom contains true emptiness and inconceivable existence as noted above, we should know that all atoms are also thus. If you realize this principle, you will find that an atom contains the ten directions with no abrogation of great and small; an instant contains the nine time frames, with extension and brevity being simultaneous. That is why we have excellent subtle words with a fine hair showing the complete teaching and why we have extraordinary holy scripture with a mote of dust manifesting the whole of being. It goes far beyond the horizons of speech and thought. It penetrates the trap of words and concepts.

The scripture says, "It is like a huge scripture, as extensive as a billion-world system, existing inside an atom, with the same being true of all atoms. If there is one person with clear wisdom, whose pure eye sees clearly in every way, he breaks open the atom and takes out the scripture for the widespread welfare of sentient beings." To speak according to the principle, the "atom" represents the false conceptions of sentient beings and the "scripture" is the complete illumination of great knowledge. Since the body of knowledge is boundless, it is said to be as extensive as a billion-world system. In accord with this teaching, it is called the universal of an atom containing emptiness and existence.

Translated by Thomas Cleary

This universe is nothing but God: what else is new? There is no need to leave the physical world behind. It's like watching a movie: the images come and go; the screen remains. But if you just want to see a blank screen, why be there at all? Pass the popcorn, please.

This universe is nothing but Brahman. See Brahman everywhere, under all circumstances, with the eye of the spirit and a tranquil heart. How can the physical eyes see anything but physical objects? How can the mind of the enlightened man think of anything other than Reality?

How could a wise man reject the experience of supreme bliss and take delight in mere outward forms? When the moon shines in its exceeding beauty, who would care to look at a painted moon?

Experience of the unreal offers us no satisfaction, nor any escape from misery. Find satisfaction, therefore, in the experience of the sweet bliss of Brahman. Devote yourself to the Atman and live happily forever.

O noble soul, this is how you must pass your days—see the Atman everywhere, fix your thought upon the Atman, the one without a second.

The Atman is one, absolute, indivisible. It is pure consciousness. To imagine many forms within it is like imagining palaces in the air. Therefore, know that you are the Atman, ever-blissful, one without a second, and find the ultimate peace. Remain absorbed in the joy which is silence.

This state of silence is a state of entire peace, in which the intellect ceases to occupy itself with the unreal. In this silence, the great soul who knows and is one with Brahman enjoys unmingled bliss forever.

To the man who has realized the Atman as his true being and who has tasted the innermost bliss of the Atman, there is no more excellent joy than this state of silence, in which all cravings are dumb.

No matter what he is doing—walking, standing, sitting, or lying down—the illumined seer whose delight is the Atman lives in joy and freedom.

When a great soul has found perfect tranquility by freeing his mind from all distracting thoughts and completely realizing Brahman, then he no longer needs sacred places, moral disciplines, set hours, postures, directions, or objects for his meditation. His knowledge of the Atman depends upon no special circumstances or conditions.

In order to know that a jar is a jar, are any special conditions required? Only that our means of perception, the eyes, shall be free from defect. This alone reveals the object.

The Atman is eternally present. It is revealed by transcendental experience, which is not dependent upon place, time, or rituals of self-purification.

I do not require any special condition or proof in order to know my own name. Similarly, for a knower of Brahman, the knowledge that "I am Brahman" does not require any proof.

The Atman, shining with its own light, causes this apparent universe. But how can anything in this universe reveal the Atman? Apart from the Atman, these appearances are worthless, bodiless, unreal.

The Vedas, the Puranas, all scriptures and all living creatures only exist because the Atman exists. How then can any of them reveal the Atman, which is the revealer of everything?

This Atman shines with its own light. Its power is infinite. It is beyond sense-knowledge. It is the source of all experience. He who knows the Atman is free from every kind of bondage. He is full of glory. He is the greatest of the great.

The things perceived by the senses cause him neither grief nor pleasure. He is not attached to them. Neither does he shun them.

Constantly delighting in the Atman, he is always at play within himself. He tastes the sweet, unending bliss of the Atman and is satisfied.

The child plays with his toys, forgetting even hunger and physical pain. In like manner, the knower of Brahman takes his delight in the Atman, forgetting all thought of "I" and "mine."

He gets his food easily by begging alms, without anxiety or care. He drinks from the clear stream. He lives unfettered and independent. He sleeps without fear in the forest or on the cremation-ground. He does not need to wash or dry his clothes, for he wears none. The earth is his bed. He walks the highway of Vedanta. His playmate is Brahman, the everlasting.

The knower of the Atman does not identify himself with his body. He rests within it, as if within a carriage. If people provide him with comforts and luxuries, he enjoys them and plays with them like a child. He bears no outward mark of a holy man. He remains quite unattached to the things of this world.

He may wear costly clothing, or none. He may be dressed in deer or tiger skin or clothed in pure knowledge. He may seem like a madman, or like a child, or sometimes like an unclean spirit. Thus he wanders the earth.

The man of contemplation walks alone. He lives desireless amidst the objects of desire. The Atman is his eternal satisfaction. He sees the Atman present in all things.

Sometimes he appears to be a fool, sometimes a wise man. Sometimes he seems splendid as a king, sometimes feeble-minded. Sometimes he is calm and silent. Sometimes he draws men to him. Sometimes people honor him greatly, sometimes they insult him. Sometimes they ignore him. That is how the illumined soul lives, always absorbed in the highest bliss.

He has no riches, yet he is always contented. He is helpless, yet of mighty power. He enjoys nothing, yet he is continually rejoicing. He has no equal, yet he sees all men as his equals.

He acts, yet is not bound by his action. He reaps the fruit of past actions, yet is unaffected by them. He has a body, but does not identify himself with it. He appears to be an individual, yet he is present in all things, everywhere.

Translated by Swami Prabhavananda and Christopher Isherwood

Short and sweet.

The Sutra says, "To behold the Buddha nature you must wait for the right moment and the right conditions. When the time comes, you are awakened as if from a dream. You realize that what you have found is your own and doesn't come from anywhere outside." An ancient patriarch said, "After enlightenment you are still the same as you were before. There is no mind and there is no truth." You are simply free from unreality and delusion. The ordinary person's mind is the same as the sage's, because Original Mind is perfect and complete in itself. When you have arrived at this recognition, please hold on to it.

The mind that dwells nowhere is the kingdom of heaven (a.k.a. the pearl of great price). Hui-hai in his kindhearted descriptions is like a mother bird who does everything for her chicks: gathers the food, chews it to a pulp, even disgorges it into their mouths.

A SPEECH TO THE ASSEMBLY

Friends and brothers, it is all right for you to be monks, but it is much better to be men unattached to all things. Why should you run around making karma that will hem you in like a criminal's chains? Trying to empty your minds, straining to attain enlightenment, blabbering about your understanding of the Buddha-Dharma—all this is a waste of energy. Once, the great Ma-tzu said to me, "Your own treasure house already contains everything you need. Why don't you use it freely, instead of chasing after something outside yourself?" From that day on, I stopped looking elsewhere. Just make use of your own treasure house according to your needs, and you will be happy men. There isn't a single thing that can be grasped or rejected. When you stop thinking that things have a past or future, and that they come or go, then in the whole universe there won't be a single atom that is not your own treasure. All you have to do is look into your own mind; then the marvelous reality will manifest itself at all times. Don't search for the truth with your intellect. Don't search at all. The nature of the mind is intrinsically pure. Thus the Flower Garland Sutra says: "All things have neither a beginning nor an end." For those who are able to interpret these words correctly, the Buddhas are always present. Furthermore, the Vimalakirti Sutra says: "Reality is perceived through your own body." If you don't run after sounds and sights, or let appearances give rise to conceptual thinking, you will become men unattached to all things. That's enough for now. Take good care of yourselves.

Question: What should the mind dwell upon?

Answer: It should dwell upon non-dwelling.

Question: What is this non-dwelling?

Answer: It means not allowing the mind to dwell upon anything whatsoever.

Question: What does that mean?

Answer: Dwelling upon nothing means that the mind doesn't remain with good or evil, being or non-being, inside or outside, emptiness or non-emptiness, concentration or distraction. This dwelling upon nothing is the state in which it should dwell; those who attain it are said to have non-dwelling minds—in other words, they have Buddha minds.

Question: What does mind resemble?

Answer: Mind has no color, is neither long nor short, doesn't appear or disappear; it is free from both purity and impurity; it was never born and can never die; it is utterly serene. This is the form of our original mind, which is also our original body.

Question: By what means does this body or mind perceive? Can it perceive with the eyes, ears, nose, touch, and consciousness?

Answer: No, there aren't several means of perception like that.

Question: Then what sort of perception is involved, since it isn't like any of the ones already mentioned?

Answer: It is perception by means of your own nature. What does this mean? Because your own nature is pure and utterly serene, its immaterial and motionless essence is capable of this perception.

Question: But since that pure essence can't be found, where does this perception come from?

Answer: We may compare it to a mirror which, though it doesn't contain any forms, can nevertheless reflect all forms. Why? Because it is free from mental activity. If your mind were clear, it wouldn't give rise to delusions, and its attachments to subject and object would vanish; then purity would arise by itself, and you would be capable of such perception. The Dharmapada Sutra says: "To establish ourselves amid perfect emptiness in a single flash is the essence of wisdom."

Question: When the mind reaches the state of not dwelling upon anything, and continues in that state, won't there be some attachment to its not dwelling upon anything?

Answer: As long as your mind dwells upon nothing, there is nothing you can attach yourself to. If you want to understand the non-dwelling mind very clearly, while you are sitting in meditation, you should be aware only of the mind and shouldn't allow yourself to make judgments—that is, you should avoid thinking in terms of good, bad, or anything else. Whatever is past is past, so don't sit in judgment upon it; for when thinking about the past disappears by itself, it can be said that there is no longer any past. Whatever is in the future hasn't arrived, so don't direct your hopes and longings toward it; for when thinking about the future disappears by itself, it can be said that there is no future. Whatever is present passes instantaneously. Just be aware of your non-attachment to everything; don't nourish any desire or aversion in your mind; for when thinking about the present disappears by itself, it can be said that there is no present. When there is no clinging to any of those three periods, it can be said that they don't exist.

If your mind wanders away, don't follow it; your mind will stop wandering by itself. If your mind lingers somewhere, don't linger with it; its search for a dwelling place will stop by itself. In this way you will come to have a non-dwelling mind—a mind that remains in the state of non-dwelling. If you are fully aware of a non-dwelling mind in yourself, you will discover that there is just the fact of dwelling, with nothing to dwell upon or not to dwell upon. This full awareness in yourself of a mind that dwells upon nothing is known as having a clear perception of your own mind or of your own true nature. A mind that dwells upon nothing is the Buddha mind, enlightenment mind, uncreated mind; it is also called realization that the nature of all appearances is unreal. It is what the sutras call "patient realization of the Uncreated." If you haven't realized it yet, please exert all your power to realize it. When you finally understand, your mind will be free from both delusion and reality. A mind that is truly free has reached the state in which opposites are seen as empty. This is the only freedom.

Even a deathbed can be the place of rebirth, as the Tibetans well know. When we open our eyes, there is no one who sees, nothing to be seen. The light is already shining.

From *The Tibetan Book of the Dead*

The method of instruction: If he is able, he will work with himself from the instructions already given. But if he cannot by himself, then his guru, or a disciple of his guru, or a Dharma-brother who was a close friend, should stay nearby and read aloud clearly the sequence of the signs of death: "Now the sign of earth dissolving into water is present, water into fire, fire into air, air into consciousness. . . ." *When the sequence is almost completed he should be encouraged to adopt an attitude like this:* "O son of noble family," *or, if he was a guru,* "O Sir,"—"do not let your thoughts wander." *This should be spoken softly in his ear. In the case of a Dharmabrother or anyone else, one should call him by name and say these words:*

"O son of noble family, that which is called death has now arrived, so you should adopt this attitude: 'I have arrived at the time of death, so now, by means of this death, I will adopt only the attitude of the enlightened state of mind, friendliness and compassion, and attain perfect enlightenment for the sake of all sentient beings as limitless as space. With this attitude, at this special time, for the sake of all sentient beings, I will recognize the luminosity of death as the Dharmakaya, and attaining in that state the supreme realization of the Great Symbol, I will act for the good of all beings. If I do not attain this, I will recognize the bardo state as it is, and attaining the indivisible Great Symbol form in the bardo, I will act for the good of all beings as limitless as space in whatever way will influence them.' Without letting go of this attitude you should remember and practice whatever meditation teaching you have received in the past."

These words should be spoken distinctly with the lips close to his ear, so as to remind him of his practice without letting his attention wander even for a moment. Then, when respiration has completely stopped, one should firmly press the arteries of sleep and remind him with these words, if he was a guru or spiritual friend higher than oneself:

"Sir, now the basic luminosity is shining before you; recognize it, and rest in the practice."

And one should show all others like this:

"O son of noble family, [name], listen. Now the pure luminosity of the Dharmata is shining before you; recognize it. O son of noble family, at this moment your state of mind is by nature pure emptiness, it does not possess any nature whatever, neither substance nor quality such as color, but it is pure emptiness; this is the Dharmata, the female Buddha Samantabhadri. But this state of mind is not just blank emptiness; it is unobstructed, sparkling, pure, and vibrant; this mind is the male Buddha Samantabhadra. These two—your mind whose nature is emptiness without any substance whatever, and your mind which is vibrant and luminous—are inseparable; this is the Dharmakaya of the Buddha. This mind of yours is inseparable luminosity and emptiness in the form of a great mass of light; it has no birth or death, therefore it is the Buddha of Immortal Light. To recognize this is all that is necessary. When you recognize this pure nature of your mind as the Buddha, looking into your own mind is resting in the Buddha-mind."

This should be repeated three or seven times, clearly and precisely. First, it will remind him of what he has previously been shown by his guru; second, he will recognize his own naked mind as the luminosity; and third, having recognized himself, he will be-

come inseparably united with the Dharmakaya and certainly attain liberation.

Translated by Francesca Fremantle and Chögyam Trungpa

———

From *The Book of the Great Liberation*

Since there is really no duality, separation is unreal. Until duality is transcended and at-one-ment realized, enlightenment cannot be attained. Both samsara and nirvana, an inseparable unity, are your own mind. It is only because of deluded ideas, which you are free to accept or reject, that you wander in the world of samsara. Practice the Dharma, grasp the essence of these teachings, and free yourself from every attachment.

When you seek your mind in its true state, you will find it quite intelligible, although it cannot be seen. In its true state, mind is naked, immaculate, transparent, empty, timeless, uncreated, unimpeded; not realizable as a separate thing, but as the unity of all things, yet not composed of them; undifferentiated, self-radiant, indivisible, and without qualities. Your own mind is not separate from other minds; it shines forth, unobscured, for all living beings.

Your own mind is originally as pure and empty as the sky. To know whether or not this is true, look inside your own mind.

Without beginning or ending, your original wisdom has been shining forever, like the sun. To know whether or not this is true, look inside your own mind.

Your original wisdom is as continuous and unstoppable as the current of a mighty river. To know whether or not this is true, look inside your own mind.

When you realize that all phenomena are as unstable as the air, they lose their power to fascinate and bind you. To know whether or not this is true, look inside your own mind.

All phenomena are your own ideas, self-conceived in the mind, like reflections in a mirror. To know whether or not this is true, look inside your own mind.

Arising spontaneously and free as the clouds in the sky, all phenomena fade away by themselves. To know whether or not this is true, look inside your own mind.

Again and again, look inside your own mind. When you look outward into the emptiness of space, you will find no place where the mind is shining. When you look into your own mind in search of the radiance, you will find nothing that shines.

This self-originated clear light is eternal and unborn. How strange and marvelous!

Since it is unborn, it cannot die. How strange and marvelous!

Although it is absolute reality, there is no one to perceive it. How strange and marvelous!

Although it wanders in samsara, it is undefiled by evil. How strange and marvelous!

Although it sees the Buddha, it is unattached to good. How strange and marvelous!

Although it is possessed by all beings, it is not recognized by them. How strange and marvelous!

Although the clear light of reality shines inside their own mind, most people look for it outside. How strange and marvelous!

Since there is nothing to meditate on, there is no meditation. Since there is nowhere you can go astray, there is no going astray. Without meditating, without going astray, look into the true state, where self-awareness, self-knowledge, self-illumination shine resplendently. This is called the enlightened mind.

These teachings are immeasurably deep and contain all wisdom. Although they are to be contemplated in a variety of ways, there are no two such things as contemplation and contemplator. When fully contemplated, these teachings merge with the seeker, although when sought the seeker himself cannot be found. Thereupon the goal of the seeking is attained, and the end of the search. At this point there is nothing more to be sought, and no need to seek anything.

Although there are no two such things as knowing and not knowing, there are profound and innumerable forms of meditation; and it is surpassingly excellent in the end to know your own mind.

Since there are no two such things as meditation and meditator, if, by those who practice or do not practice meditation, the meditator is sought and not found, thereupon the goal of meditation is reached and also the end of meditation itself.

Since there are no two such things as meditation and object of meditation, there is no need to fall under the sway of ignorance; for as the result of meditation on the original serenity of the mind, the uncreated wisdom instantaneously shines forth.

Although there is an innumerable variety of profound practices, they do not exist for your mind in its true state; for there are no two such things as existence and non-existence.

Since there are no two such things as practice and practitioner, if, by those who practice or do not practice, the practitioner of practice is sought and not found, thereupon the goal of practice is reached and also the end of the practice itself.

The uncreated, self-radiant wisdom of your original mind, actionless, immaculate, transcendent over acceptance and rejection, is itself the perfect practice.

Mind is everything; mind is nothing. Mind creates time and space, mind contains a billion galaxies, mind lifts a spoon of oatmeal to its mouth at breakfast. Mind is life and death, God and devil, you and I; mind stands at the top of the mountain; mind cries for its mother's breast. Mind pulls the universe out of a top hat, bows to its own applause, and walks off the stage, grinning.

All Buddhas and all ordinary beings are nothing but the one mind. This mind is beginningless and endless, unborn and indestructible. It has no color or shape, neither exists nor doesn't exist, isn't old or new, long or short, large or small, since it transcends all measures, limits, names, and comparisons. It is what you see in front of you. Start to think about it and immediately you are mistaken. It is like the boundless void, which can't be fathomed or measured. The one mind is the Buddha, and there is no distinction between Buddha and ordinary beings, except that ordinary beings are attached to forms and thus seek for Buddhahood outside themselves. By this very seeking they lose it, since they are using Buddha to seek for Buddha, using mind to seek for mind. Even if they continue for a million eons, they will never be able to find it. They don't know that all they have to do is put a stop to conceptual thinking, and the Buddha will appear before them, because this mind is the Buddha and the Buddha is all living beings. It is not any less for being manifested in ordinary beings, nor any greater for being manifested in Buddhas.

———

This pure mind, which is the source of all things, shines forever with the radiance of its own perfection. But most people are not aware of it, and think that mind is just the faculty that sees, hears, feels, and knows. Blinded by their own sight, hearing, feeling, and knowing, they don't perceive the radiance of the source. If they could eliminate all conceptual thinking, this source would appear, like the sun rising through the empty sky and illuminating the whole universe. Therefore, you students of the Tao who seek to understand through seeing, hearing, feeling, and knowing, when your perceptions are cut off, your way to mind will be cut off and you will find nowhere to enter. Just realize that although mind is manifested in these perceptions, it is neither part of them nor separate from them. You shouldn't try to analyze these perceptions, or think about them at all; but you shouldn't seek the one mind apart from them. Don't hold on to them or leave them behind or dwell in them or reject them. Above, below, and around you, all things spontaneously exist, because there is nowhere outside the Buddha mind.

———

When most people hear that the Buddhas transmit the teaching of the one mind, they suppose that there is something to be attained or realized apart from mind, and they use mind to seek the teaching, not realizing that mind and the object of their search are one. Mind can't be used to seek mind; if it is, even after millions of eons have gone by, the search will still not be over. Suppose that a warrior forgot he was already wearing his pearl on his forehead, and sought for it somewhere else: he might search through the whole world without finding it. But if someone simply pointed it out to him, the warrior would immediately realize that the pearl had been there all the time. In the same way, if you students of the Tao are mistaken about your own mind, not recognizing that it is the Buddha, you will look for it somewhere else, indulging in various practices and hoping to attain something. But even after eons of diligent searching, you won't be able to attain the Tao. These methods can't be compared to the elimination of conceptual thinking, when you understand there is nothing that has absolute existence, nothing to hold on to, nothing to depend on, nothing to dwell in, nothing subjective or objective. When you prevent the rise of conceptual thinking, you will be free men, and this just means you will realize that the Buddha has always existed in your own mind. Eons of striving will turn out to be wasted effort; just as, when the warrior found his pearl, he simply found what had been hanging on his forehead all the time, and his discovery had nothing to do with his efforts to find it elsewhere. Therefore the Buddha said, "I didn't attain a single thing through Supreme Perfect Enlightenment." It was because he was concerned that people wouldn't believe this that he taught by less direct methods. This statement of his isn't idle chatter; it expresses the highest truth.

———

Your true nature is not lost in moments of delusion, nor is it gained at the moment of enlightenment. It was never born and can never die. It shines through the whole universe, filling emptiness, one with emptiness. It is without time or space, and has no passions, actions, ignorance, or knowledge. In it there are no things, no people, and no Buddhas; it contains not the smallest hairbreadth of anything that exists objectively; it depends on nothing and is attached to nothing. It is all-pervading, radiant beauty: absolute reality, self-existent and uncreated. How then can you doubt that the Buddha has no mouth to speak with and nothing to teach, or that the truth is learned without learning, for who is there to learn? It is a jewel beyond all price.

———

When a thought suddenly flashes in your mind and you recognize its illusory nature, then you can enter into the state of all the Buddhas of the past—not that the Buddhas of the past really exist, or that the Buddhas of the future have not yet come into existence. Above all, don't wish to become a future Buddha; your only concern should be, as thought follows thought, to avoid clinging to any of them. Nor should you wish to be a Buddha right now. If a Buddha arises, cut him off instantly. Don't cling to him for even a single moment, because a thousand locks couldn't shut him in, nor a hundred thousand feet of rope bind him.

I will now explain how to free yourselves of that Buddha. Consider the sunlight. You may say that it is near, yet if you pursue it from world to world you will never catch it. You may say that it is far, yet you can see it right before your eyes. Chase it and it always eludes you; run from it and it is always there. From this example you can understand how it is with the true nature of all things, and from now on there will be no need to grieve or worry about such things.

Now, please don't think that when I said you should cut off the Buddha I was being profane, or that when I compared him to the sunlight I was being pious. In Zen we don't admit either the profanity of the first or the piety of the second. Nor do we think that the first is Buddha-like and the second ignorant.

The entire visible universe is the Buddha; so are all sounds. Hold fast to one principle and all the others are identical. On seeing one thing, you see all things. On perceiving any individual's mind, you perceive all mind. Glimpse one truth, and all truth is present in your vision, for there is nowhere at all which is devoid of the Truth. When you see a grain of sand, you see all possible worlds, with all their vast rivers and mountains. When you see a drop of water, you see the nature of all the waters of the universe. Furthermore, in thus contemplating the totality of phenomena, you are contemplating the totality of mind. All these phenomena are intrinsically empty, yet this mind they are identical with is not mere nothingness. It does exist, but in a way too marvelous for us to comprehend. It is an existence that is beyond existence, a non-existence that is nevertheless existence.

Thus we can encompass all possible worlds, numberless as grains of sand, with our one mind. Then why talk of "inside" and "outside"? Since honey is naturally characterized by sweetness, it follows that all honey is sweet. To speak of this honey as sweet and that honey as bitter would be ridiculous. That is why we say that emptiness has no inside or outside. It arises by itself, spontaneous and absolute.

Ordinary beings are the Buddha, just as they are. The Buddha is one with them. Both have the same nature. The phenomenal universe and nirvana, activity and stillness—all have the same nature. So do all possible worlds and the state that transcends all worlds. The beings that pass through the six stages of existence, those who have undergone the four kinds of birth, all the worlds with their vast mountains and rivers, enlightenment and delusion—all of them are the same. When I say that they all have the same nature, I mean that their names and forms, their existence and non-existence, are empty. The vast world-systems, uncountable as the sands of the Ganges, are all contained in the one boundless, empty, radiant mind. How then can there be Buddhas who save or ordinary beings who must be saved? If the true nature of all things is the same, how can such distinctions be real?

Do you want to know how clear a spiritual teacher is? See how invested she is in being a teacher, and how honest she is with herself. Clarity means straightforwardness. That is why the Master has been compared to a clam: as soon as she opens her mouth, you can see her intestines.

The mind of a Zen Master is perfectly straightforward. He has neither front nor back and is without deceit or delusion. Every hour of the day, what he hears and sees are ordinary sights and sounds, but nothing is distorted. He is perfectly unattached to things, and thus doesn't need to shut his eyes and ears. Because he has eliminated delusion, perverted views, and bad thinking habits, he is as clear and tranquil as an autumn stream. Someone who is like this is called a Master of Zen, a man who has freed himself from all attachments.

The path of love and the path of insight lead into the same garden.

When love is established in the heart of a servant of God, there is no place there for remembrance of men or demons or of Paradise or Hell, or for anything except the remembrance of the Beloved and his grace. The love of God in its essence is the illumination of the heart by joy because of its nearness to the Beloved, for love, in solitude, rises up triumphant, and the heart of the lover is possessed by the sense of its fellowship with him, and when solitude is combined with secret intercourse with the Beloved, the joy of that intercourse overwhelms the mind, so that it is no longer concerned with this world and what is in it.

To the one whom God has placed in the rank of his lovers, he gives the vision of himself, for he has sworn, "By my glory, I will show him my face, and I will heal his soul by the vision of myself." The hearts of such lovers are held captive in the hidden shrine of the divine lovingkindness; they are marked out by their knowledge of the revelation of the divine majesty, being transformed by the joy of the vision, in contemplation of the invisible and of the enveloping glory of God, and from them all hindrances are removed, for they tread the path of friendship with God and are transported into the garden of vision, and their hearts dwell in that region, where they see without eyes, and are in the company of the Beloved without looking upon him, and converse with an unseen friend.

This is the description of the lovers of God, who do righteousness, who are gifted with heavenly wisdom, who are on their guard both night and day, pure in all their thoughts, those whom God has prepared for his service, whom he has preserved by his care, whom he has invested with his own authority. They are continually serving him to whom the heavens and the earth belong; they are completely satisfied, for they live the good life, their bliss is eternal and their joy is made perfect and they possess an everlasting treasure within their hearts, for it is as if they contemplated with the eye of the heart the glory that is invisible, and God is the object and goal of their aspirations. Whoever knows God loves him, and whoever loves him he brings to dwell with him, and whomever he brings to dwell with him, in whom he dwells, blessed is he, yes, blessed is he.

Translated by Margaret Smith

Why is it that we become more humble as we become more like God? "From within or from behind," Emerson wrote, "a light shines through us upon things and makes us aware that we are nothing, but the light is all." Compassion is another name for clarity.

The saint becomes more humble every hour, for every hour he draws nearer to God. The saints see without knowledge, without sight, without information received, without observation, without description, without veiling, and without veil. They are not themselves, but insofar as they exist at all, they exist in God. Their movements are caused by God, and their words are the words of God, which are uttered by their tongues, and their sight is the sight of God, which has entered into their eyes. So God Most High has said, "When I love a servant, I am his ear, so that he hears by me; I am his eye, so that he sees by me; and I am his tongue, so that he speaks by me."

The saints are those whom God has invested with the radiance of his love and adorned with the mantle of his grace; he set the crown of his joy upon their heads, and he put love for them into the hearts of his creatures. Then he brought them forth, having entrusted to their hearts the treasures of the invisible, which depend upon union with the Beloved, and their hearts are turned toward him, and their eyes behold the greatness of his majesty. Then he made them seek for a remedy, and he let them know where the means of healing was to be found. He caused their disciples to be abstinent and God-fearing, and to them, his saints, he gave assurance of an answer to their prayers, and he said: "O my saints, if you meet someone who is sick through separation from me, heal him; or if he is a fugitive from me, seek him out; or if he is afraid of me, reassure him; or if he desires union with me, show him favor; or if he seeks to approach me, encourage him. If he despairs of my grace, help him; or if he hopes for my lovingkindness, give him good news; or if he has right thoughts of me, welcome him; or if he shows love to me, be kind to him; or if he seeks to know my attributes, give him guidance; or if he does evil in spite of my lovingkindness, remonstrate with him; or if he is forgetful of it, remind him. If anyone who is injured asks help of you, give it to him; and if anyone joins you in my name, show friendship; if he goes astray, search for him; but if he wants to make you sin, put him away from you. O my saints, I have reasoned with you, and to you I have addressed myself, from you I have sought the fulfillment of my will, for upon you my choice has been placed, and I have predestined you for my work. I have appointed you to serve me, and I have chosen you to be my elect. To you I have given the most precious of rewards, the most beautiful of gifts, the greatest of graces. I am the searcher of hearts, he who knows the mysteries of the invisible. I am the object of your desire, I who read the secrets of the heart. You are my saints, my beloved: you are mine and I am yours."

Translated by Margaret Smith

The authorities crucified the Sufi ancestor al-Hallaj for declaring "I am the Truth." They were looking at the stars through the wrong end of a telescope. Hallaj let out a loud laugh and died. Any of his descendants would have done the same, especially Abu Yazid, the prince of Sufis. Does a diamond let itself be cut by glass? Does a pearl refuse to glisten when cast before swine?

Nothing is better for a man than to be without anything, having no asceticism, no theory, no practice. When he is without everything, he is with everything.

———

For a long time I used to circumambulate the Kaaba. When I attained God, I saw the Kaaba circumambulating me.

———

I sloughed off my self as a snake sloughs off its skin. Then I looked into myself and saw that I am He.

———

Anyone whose reward from God is deferred until tomorrow has not truly worshiped Him today.

———

Be in a realm where neither good nor evil exists. Both of them belong to the world of created beings; in the presence of Unity there is neither command nor prohibition.

———

He was asked, "What is the way to God?" He answered, "Leave the way and you have arrived at God."

———

For thirty years God was my mirror, now I am my own mirror. What I was I no longer am, for "I" and "God" are a denial of God's unity. Since I no longer am, God is his own mirror. He speaks with my tongue, and I have vanished.

———

A single atom of the sweetness of wisdom in a man's heart is better than a thousand pavilions in Paradise.

———

Men learn from the dead, but I learn from the Living One who never dies. All the rest speak to God, but I speak *from* God.

———

This thing we tell of can never be found by seeking, yet only seekers find it.

———

For thirty years I used to say, "Do this" and "Give that"; but when I reached the first stage of wisdom, I said, "O God, be mine and do whatever You want."

———

Forgetfulness of self is remembrance of God. Whoever knows God through God becomes alive, and whoever knows God through self becomes dead.

———

I went from God to God, until they cried from me in me, "O Thou
I!"

———

Try to gain one moment in which you see only God in heaven and
earth.

———

All this talk and turmoil and noise and movement and desire is outside the veil; inside the veil is silence and calm and peace.

Translated by Reynold A. Nicholson

JOHANNES SCOTUS ERIGENA (C. 810–C. 877)

God is the source, the well of creation, natura naturans, *the mother of the universe: unknowable, unthinkable, unnamable, yet at every moment inexhaustibly present. But if we start imagining God as behind the world, or beyond, or prior, or separate in any way, we have already stirred up mud in the clear water.*

How can there be any place not filled with the glory of God? Once we step out of the self, distinctions fall away, and we see God everywhere: in the rosebush, in the dirt, in the screaming of the neighbor's kids, in the laundry on the clothesline.

> *If I rise to heaven, I meet you;*
> *if I lie down in hell, you are there.*
> *If I plunge through the fear of the terrorist*
> *or pierce through the rapist's rage,*
> *you are there, in your infinite compassion,*
> *and my heart rejoices in your joy.*

We ought not to understand God and creation as two things distinct from each other, but as one and the same. For both the creature, by subsisting, is in God; and God, by manifesting himself, in a marvelous and ineffable manner creates himself in the creature, the invisible making himself visible, and the incomprehensible comprehensible, and the hidden revealed, and the unknown known, and what is without form and species formed and specific, and the superessential essential, and the supernatural natural, and the simple composite, and the accident-free subject to accident, and the infinite finite, and the uncircumscribed circumscribed, and the supertemporal temporal, and the creator of all things created in all things, and the maker of all things made in all things; and eternal he begins to be, and immobile he moves into all things and becomes all things in all things.

Translated by I. P. Sheldon-Williams

———

The term "nothing" signifies the ineffable, incomprehensible, and inaccessible brilliance of the divine goodness, which is unknown to all intellects, whether human or angelic, because it is superessential and supernatural. This term is applied, I think, because when the divine goodness is thought through itself, it neither is nor was nor will be. For in no existing thing is it understood, since it is beyond all things. But when, through a certain ineffable descent into the things that are, the divine goodness is perceived by the sight of the mind in those things that are, it alone is found to be in all things, and it is and was and shall be. Therefore when it is understood as incomprehensible on account of its excellence, it is not improperly called "nothing." But when it begins to appear in its theophanies, it is said to proceed as though from nothing into something. What is properly judged to be above all essence is also known properly in every essence, and for this reason every visible and invisible creature can be called a theophany, that is, a divine appearance.

———

The divine nature is created and creates in the primordial causes; but in their effects it is created and does not create. And not without reason, since in these effects it establishes the end of its descent, that is, of its appearance. In the scriptures, therefore, every corporeal and visible creature which falls under the senses is generally called—and not inappropriately—an outermost trace of the divine nature.

———

Translated by Donald F. Duclow

Yun-men is one of the great teachers. He goes right to the essence, right for the jugular. Look out!

Let me take the whole universe and put it on the tips of your eyelashes. Don't be impatient when you hear this, but slowly and carefully examine it. If you are a good student, you won't rest until you have realized it. Then you will be a superior person; when you hear that some great Master has appeared in the world to liberate all beings, you'll immediately clap your hands over your ears. As long as you aren't your own Master, you may think you have gained something from what you hear; but it is secondhand merchandise, and not yours.

Look at Te-shan. The moment he saw a monk coming, he would chase him off with his stick. Or Mu-chou: whenever a monk entered his room, he would say, "You deserve to be hit thirty times." What can other teachers do? If they don't know for themselves, they are just swallowing other people's saliva. Brothers, those who really have it live like ordinary men. Those who don't have it should use their time. Be very careful.

Among the ancient Masters, there are quite a few who left helpful teachings. Hsueh-feng, for example, said, "The whole earth is nothing but you." Chia-shan said, "Find me on the tips of a hundred blades of grass, and recognize the king in a crowded market." Lo-p'u said, "When you hold a grain of dust, you are holding the universe in your hand. A golden lion, in all its splendor, is you." Take these teachings and meditate on them, again and again; someday you will find your entrance. But no one can do it for you. Every one of you should work toward self-realization. The Master can only bear testimony. If you have gained something within, he can't hide it from you; if you haven't gained anything, he can't find it for you.

80

Brothers, time waits for no man. If you should get fatally sick before you realize the truth, what would you do? Wouldn't you be like a crab that has fallen into boiling water, its legs flailing in confusion and pain? So don't waste your time. Life is precious; if you miss this chance, it may take a billion eons before you receive a human body again. If even a worldly man like Confucius said, "He who realizes the Tao in the morning can die content in the evening," how much more effort should we monks put into this matter! Please do your best, and take good care of yourselves.

The Japanese Zen Master Bankei said, "The farther you enter into the truth, the deeper it is."

When a man walks into the sea up to his knees or waist, he can see the water all around him. But when he dives into the water, he can no longer see anything outside, and he knows only that his whole body is in the water. This is what happens to those who plunge into the vision of God.

———

The more a man enters the light of understanding, the more aware he is of his own ignorance. And when the light reveals itself fully and unites with him and draws him into itself, so that he finds himself alone in a sea of light, then he is emptied of all knowledge and immersed in absolute unknowing.

———

Our mind is pure and simple. When it is emptied of thought, it enters the pure and simple light of God, and finds nothing but the light.

This sheikh is among the loveliest and most mature of Sufis. Whether he is
speaking of the wisdom that "cannot be sewed on with needle or tied on
with thread" or of the friends of God, whose souls "know one another by
smell, like horses," his words breathe genuineness through every pore.

You are freed from your own desires when God frees you. This is
not effected by your own exertion, but by the grace of God. First
he brings forth in you the desire to attain this goal. Then he opens
to you the gate of repentance. Then he throws you into self-
mortification, so that you continue to strive and, for a while, to
pride yourself upon your efforts, thinking that you are advancing or
achieving something; but afterward you fall into despair and feel
no joy. Then you know that your work is not pure but tainted, you
repent of the acts of devotion which you had thought were your
own, and perceive that they were done by God's grace and that you
were guilty of polytheism in attributing them to your own exertion.
When this becomes manifest, a feeling of joy enters your heart.
Then God opens to you the gate of certainty, so that for a time you
accept anything from anyone and endure contumely and abase-
ment, and know for certain who caused this, and doubt concerning
it is removed from your heart. Then God opens to you the gate of
love, and here too egoism shows itself for a time and you are ex-
posed to blame, which means that in your love of God you meet
fearlessly whatever may befall you and reproach does not touch
you. But still you think "I love" and find no rest until you perceive
that it is God who loves you and keeps you in the state of loving, and
that this is the result of divine love and grace, not of your own endeavor. Then God opens to you the gate of unity and causes you to
know that all action depends on God Almighty. Hereupon you perceive that all is God, and all is by him, and all is his, that he has laid

this self-conceit upon his creatures in order to prove them, and that he in his omnipotence ordains that they shall hold this false belief, because omnipotence is his attribute, so that when they regard his attributes they shall know that he is the Lord. What formerly was hearsay now becomes known to you intuitively as you contemplate the works of God. Then you entirely recognize that you do not have the right to say "I" or "mine." At this stage you behold your helplessness; desires fall away from you and you become free and calm. You desire what God desires; your own desires are gone, you are emancipated from your wants, and have gained peace and joy in both worlds.

First, action is necessary, then knowledge, in order that you may know that you know nothing and are no one. This is not easy to know. It is a thing that cannot be rightly learned by instruction, nor sewed on with needle nor tied on with thread. It is the gift of God.

———

Four thousand years before God created these bodies, he created the souls and kept them beside himself and shed a light upon them. He knew what quantity of light each soul received and he showed favor to each in proportion to its illumination. The souls remained all that time in the light, until they became fully nourished. Those who in this world live in joy and agreement with one another must have been akin to one another in that place. Here they love one another and are called the friends of God, and they are brothers who love one another for God's sake. These souls know one another by smell, like horses. Though one be in the East and the other in the West, they still feel joy and comfort in each other's talk, and one who lives in a later generation than the other is instructed and consoled by the words of his friend.

Translated by Reynold A. Nicholson

———

If men wish to draw near to God, they must seek him in the hearts of men. They should speak well of all men, whether present or absent, and if they themselves seek to be a light to guide others, then, like the sun, they must show the same face to all. To bring joy to a single heart is better than to build many shrines for worship, and to enslave one soul by kindness is worth more than setting free a thousand slaves.

The true man of God sits in the midst of his fellow-men, and rises and eats and sleeps and marries and buys and sells and gives and takes in the bazaars and spends the days with other people, and yet never forgets God even for a single moment.

Translated by Margaret Smith

Do good; avoid evil. That is the first step in all religions. The theory is simple; but the practice is difficult; then the practice itself becomes simple. It is like watching a great tennis player or a great pianist: everything looks breathtakingly natural, as if we could walk out onto the court or sit down at the piano and do the same thing. The Master makes everything seem easy; but she has put an immense effort into achieving this effortlessness.

When the light of understanding dawns in the soul and shows her how ignominious were all the former objects of her love, her eyes are opened and her vision of God becomes clear. And when she realizes God's infinite goodness, she bows down before him in fear and great awe and will not stand until the Blessed One himself comes to reassure her and lift her up. Then she drinks deeply out of the cup of God's love, and her great thirst for him is satisfied, and she enjoys the bliss of being alone with God, devoting herself entirely to him, loving him, and trusting him completely. Every action she performs is for his sake. Every thought she has is of him. Every word she utters, every song she sings, is in remembrance of him, in praise of him, in love of him. If he bestows a benefit on her, she is grateful. If he afflicts her, she suffers patiently, and her love for him only grows. It is said of one of our lovers of God that he used to rise at night and say, "Dear Lord, you have made me endure hunger, left me naked, and plunged me into deep darkness. In all this you have shown me your power and goodness. If you were to burn my body in the fire, it would only increase my love for you and my joy in you." This is like what Job said: "Though he kill me, yet will I trust in him." And the wise Solomon hinted at the same feeling when he said, "My beloved is a bundle of myrrh lying between my breasts." Our sages explain this as follows: "Even if he makes me suffer bitterness like myrrh, nevertheless he lies on my heart, between my breasts."

86

He who trusts in God is able to remove his attention from worldly anxieties and devote it entirely to doing what is right. For in the peace of his soul and the liberty of his mind, and in the disappearance of his anxieties about worldly matters, he is like an alchemist who knows how to turn tin into silver and silver into gold. But he is better off: for he requires neither implements nor materials in his alchemy, and he doesn't need to hide his gold in fear of robbers, or restrict his production to what is only enough for today and be anxious about tomorrow. For he trusts with his whole heart that God will provide whatever he needs.

If he who trusts in God is rich, he will cheerfully fulfill all the religious and ethical obligations that a rich man has; and if he is poor, he will consider the absence of money as a blessing from God, relieving him of the responsibilities its possession involves, and from the labor of guarding and managing it. The rich man who trusts in God will not find his wealth an obstacle to his faith; for he doesn't place his confidence in his wealth, which is for him a trust he has been assigned for a limited period so that he may apply it for the good of himself, his family, and his society. He doesn't take credit for his generosity, nor does he give charity or do good deeds except anonymously, or require any reward or praise; but in his heart he gives thanks to the Creator who has made him the agent of His beneficence. And if he loses his wealth, he doesn't worry or mourn its loss, but is grateful to God for taking away what was only entrusted to him, just as he was grateful to God for the original gift, and he rejoices in his portion.

The Tao is hidden but always present. It is hidden because we can't perceive it with our senses or know it with our intellect. But if we live it, we can feel its presence in our life, like the traces of a subatomic particle in a cloud chamber. When we fully surrender our ego-bound past and future, there is nothing but the present: nothing but presence.

All beauty is loved by those who are able to perceive beauty, for the perception of beauty is a delight in itself. Beautiful forms are loved for themselves and not for any end to be obtained from them, and this cannot be denied: for instance, green plants and running water are loved for themselves, not for the sake of drinking the water or eating the plants. So too with trees and flowers and birds: the very sight of them is a joy, and all joy is loved. It cannot be denied that where beauty is perceived it is natural to love it, and if it is certain that God is beauty, he must be loved by those to whom his beauty and his majesty are revealed. In God and in him alone are all these causes combined and all things lovable found in their highest perfection. For it is to him that man owes his very existence and the qualities by which he may attain to his perfection. He is the only real benefactor and the ultimate cause of all benefits. If, where beauty is found, it is natural to love it, and if all beauty consists in perfection, then it follows that the All-Beautiful, who is absolute perfection, must be loved by those to whom his nature and attributes are revealed.

Finally, man loves God because of the affinity between the human soul and its source, for it shares in the divine nature and attributes, because through knowledge and love it can attain to eternal life and itself become Godlike. Such love, when it has grown strong and overwhelming, is called passion, which is love firmly established and limitless. It is reasonable to give this passionate love to that One from whom all good things are seen to come. In truth, there is nothing good or beautiful or beloved in this world that does not come from his lovingkindness and is not the gift of his grace, a draught from the sea of his bounty. For all that is good and just and lovely in the world, perceived by the intellect and the sight and the hearing and the rest of the senses, from the creation of the world until it shall pass away, from the summit of the Pleiades to the ends of the earth, is just a particle from the treasure of his riches and a ray from the splendor of his glory. Is it not reasonable to love him who is thus described, and is it not comprehensible that those who have mystic knowledge of his attributes should love him more and more until their love passes all bounds? To use the term "passion" for it is indeed wrong, for it fails to express the greatness of their love for him.

Glory be to him, who is concealed from sight by the brightness of his light. If he had not veiled himself with seventy veils of light, the splendors of his countenance would surely consume the eyes of those who contemplate the beauty which is his.

———

When the mystic enters into the pure and absolute unicity of the One and into the kingdom of the One and Alone, mortals reach the end of their ascent. For there is no ascent beyond it, since ascent involves multiplicity, and implies an ascent from somewhere to somewhere, and when multiplicity has been eliminated, unity is established and relationship ceases, signs are effaced, there remains neither height nor depth, nor anyone to descend or ascend. No higher ascent is possible for the soul, for there is no height beyond the highest and no multiplicity in the face of unity, and since multiplicity has been effaced, no further ascent.

Those who have passed into the unitive life have attained to a being transcending all that can be apprehended by sight or insight, for they find that God transcends in his sanctity everything we have

89

described. But these can be separated into classes. For some of them, all that can be perceived is consumed away, blotted out, annihilated, but the soul remains contemplating that supreme beauty and holiness and contemplating itself in the beauty it has acquired by attaining to the divine presence, and for such a one, things seen are blotted out, but not the seeing soul. But some pass beyond this, and they are the elect of the elect, who are consumed by the glory of his exalted face, and the greatness of the divine majesty overwhelms them and they are annihilated and they themselves are no more. They no longer contemplate themselves, and there remains only the One, the Real, and the meaning of his word "All things perish except his face" is known by experience.

This is the final degree of those who attain, but some of them in their ascent did not follow the gradual process we have described, nor was the ascent long for them. At the very beginning, outstripping their compeers, they attained to a knowledge of the All-Holy and the divine transcendence. They were overcome at the first by what overcame others at the last. The divine epiphany broke in upon them all at once, so that all things perceptible by sight or by insight were consumed in the glory of his face.

Ask that I may be forgiven if my pen has gone astray or my foot has slipped, for to plunge into the abyss of the divine mysteries is a perilous thing, and it is no easy task to seek to discover the unclouded glory that lies behind the veil.

Translated by Margaret Smith

The single word before sound, the word that was in the beginning, the word that sings in the womb of space: is it a word, really? Can all the eloquence on earth conceive or convey it? And when you have killed the Buddha and left the saints sobbing at his funeral, what have you come to, after all? Hello . . . Goodbye . . . I love you . . . Have a nice day . . .

The thousand sages have not transmitted the single word before sound; if you have never seen it personally, it's as if it were worlds away. Even if you discern it before sound and cut off the tongues of everyone in the world, you're still not a sharp fellow. Therefore it is said, "The sky can't cover it; the earth can't support it; empty space can't contain it; sun and moon can't illumine it." Where there is no Buddha and you alone are called the Honored One, for the first time you've amounted to something. Otherwise, if you are not yet this way, penetrate through on the tip of a hair and release the great shining illumination; then in all directions you will be independent and free in the midst of phenomena; whatever you pick up, there is nothing that's not it. But tell me, what is attained that is so extraordinary?

———

If you understand, you can make use of it on the road, like a dragon reaching the water, like a tiger in the mountains. If you don't understand, then the worldly truth will prevail, and you will be like a ram caught in a fence, like a fool watching over a stump waiting for a rabbit. Sometimes a single phrase is like a lion crouching on the ground; sometimes a phrase is like the Diamond King's jewel sword. Sometimes a phrase cuts off the tongues of everyone on earth, and sometimes a phrase follows the waves and pursues the currents.

If you make use of it on the road, when you meet with a man of knowledge you distinguish what's appropriate to the occasion, you know what's right and what's wrong, and together you witness each other's illumination. Where the worldly truth prevails, one who has the single eye can cut off everything in the ten directions and stand like a mile-high wall. Therefore it is said, "When the great function appears, it does not keep to any fixed standards." Sometimes we take a blade of grass and use it as the sixteen-foot golden body; sometimes we take the sixteen-foot golden body and use it as a blade of grass. But tell me, what principle does this depend upon? Do you really know?

Translated by Thomas and J. C. Cleary

The way down is the way up; the way in is the way out.

When we lift up the eyes of the mind to what is invisible, we should consider metaphors of visible things as if they were steps to understanding. Therefore, in spiritual matters, when something is called "the highest," this doesn't mean that it is located above the top of the heavens, but rather that it is the inmost or most intimate of all. Thus, to ascend to God is to enter into oneself, and not only to enter into oneself, but, in some unsayable manner, in the inmost parts to pass beyond oneself. He who can, as it were, enter into himself and, going deeper and deeper, pass beyond himself, truly ascends to God. But when a man, through the senses of his flesh, goes out to visible things, desiring what is transitory and perishable, he descends from the dignity of his natural condition to what is unworthy of his desire. For what is inmost is nearest and highest and eternal; and what is outside is lowest and distant and transitory. So to return from the outside to the inmost is to ascend from the lowest to the highest and to gather oneself from a state of scatteredness and confusion. Since we truly know that this world is outside us and that God is within us, when we return from the world to God and, as it were, lift ourselves up from what is lowest, we must pass through ourselves. Thus, when we turn from outer, perishable things, it is as if we were sailing over the waves, until we find the calm that is inside us. Happy is he who escapes unharmed from that storm-tossed sea, and reaches the safety of the port!

This is the most famous koan in Zen: an excellent way to be cast into the inner darkness, with no gnashing of teeth. Koans are meant to cause the creative impasse that any of life's natural dilemmas can be. If we have the courage and patience to remain in not-knowing, then eventually the solution falls into our lap, like a ripe fruit.

THE GATELESS BARRIER, CASE 1

A monk asked Chao-chou, "Has the dog Buddha-nature or not?" Chao-chou said, "Mu."

For the practice of Zen it is imperative that you pass through the barrier set up by the Ancestral Teachers. For subtle realization it is of the utmost importance that you cut off the mind road. If you do not pass the barrier of the ancestors, if you do not cut off the mind road, then you are a ghost clinging to bushes and grasses.

What is the barrier of the Ancestral Teachers? It is just this one word "Mu"—the one barrier of our faith. We call it the Gateless Barrier of the Zen tradition. When you pass through this barrier, you will not only interview Chao-chou intimately. You will walk hand in hand with all the Ancestral Teachers in the successive generations of our lineage—the hair of your eyebrows entangled with theirs, seeing with the same eyes, hearing with the same ears. Won't that be fulfilling? Is there anyone who would not want to pass this barrier?

So, then, make your whole body a mass of doubt, and with your three hundred and sixty bones and joints and your eighty-four thousand hair follicles concentrate on this one word "Mu." Day and night, keep digging into it. Don't consider it to be nothingness. Don't think in terms of "has" and "has not." It is like swallowing a red-hot iron ball. You try to vomit it out, but you can't.

Gradually you purify yourself, eliminating mistaken knowledge and attitudes you have held from the past. Inside and outside become one. You're like a mute person who has had a dream—you know it for yourself alone.

Suddenly Mu breaks open. The heavens are astonished, the earth is shaken. It is as though you have snatched the great sword of General Kuan. When you meet the Buddha, you kill the Buddha. When you meet Bodhidharma, you kill Bodhidharma. At the very cliff edge of birth-and-death, you find the Great Freedom. In the Six Worlds and in the Four Modes of Birth, you enjoy a samadhi of frolic and play.

How, then, should you work with it? Exhaust all your life energy on this one word "Mu." If you do not falter, then it's done! A single spark lights your Dharma candle.

Translated by Robert Aitken

The first of the following essays is one of the most profound and beautiful prose pieces ever written.

The second is a set of specific instructions for formal daily practice, which is an essential commitment for those who wish to study the self: to forget the self and be enlightened by all things.

THE MANIFESTATION OF THE TRUTH

When all things exist, there are enlightenment and delusion, practice, life and death, Buddhas and ordinary people. When all things are without self, there is no delusion, no enlightenment, no Buddhas, no ordinary people, no life and no death. Buddhism is beyond being and non-being; so there are life and death, delusion and enlightenment, ordinary people and Buddhas. Thus, when flowers fall we are sad, and when weeds grow we are annoyed.

To start from the self and try to understand all things is delusion. To let the self be awakened by all things is enlightenment. To be enlightened about delusion is to be a Buddha. To be deluded in the midst of enlightenment is to be an ordinary person. Then there are those who are enlightened beyond enlightenment, and those who are deluded by delusion. When Buddhas are truly Buddhas, they don't need to be aware of themselves as Buddhas. But they are enlightened ones. They advance in enlightenment.

When we see forms or hear sounds with our whole body and mind, we understand them intimately. But it isn't like images in a mirror or the moon reflected in water. When we look at one side, the other is dark.

To study Buddhism is to study the self. To study the self is to forget the self. To forget the self is to be enlightened by all things. To be enlightened by all things is to drop off our own body and mind, and to drop off the bodies and minds of others. No trace of enlightenment remains, and this no-trace continues endlessly.

When we first seek the truth, we think we are far from it. When we discover that the truth is already in us, we are all at once our original self. If we watch the shore from a boat, it seems that the shore is moving. But when we watch the boat directly, we know it is the boat that is moving. If we look at the world with a deluded body and mind, we will think that our self is permanent. But if we practice correctly and return to our true self, we will realize that nothing is permanent.

Wood burns and there are ashes; the process is never reversed. But we shouldn't think that what is now ashes was once wood. We should understand that wood is at the stage of wood, and that is where we find its before and after. There is a past and a future, but its present is independent of them. Ashes are at the stage of ashes, and that is where we find their before and after. Just as wood doesn't become wood again after it has turned into ashes, a person doesn't return to life after death.

Thus it is taught in Buddhism that life doesn't become death. For this reason, life is called the Unborn. It is also taught that death doesn't become life. So death is called the Undying.

Life is complete in itself; death is complete in itself. They are like the seasons. We don't call spring the future summer, or winter the past of spring.

Gaining enlightenment is like the moon reflected on the water. The moon doesn't get wet; the water isn't broken. Although its light is broad and great, the moon is reflected even in a puddle an inch wide. The whole moon and the whole sky are reflected in one dewdrop on the grass.

Enlightenment doesn't destroy the person, just as the moon doesn't break the water. The person doesn't hinder enlightenment, just as a dewdrop doesn't hinder the moon in the sky. The depth of the dewdrop is the height of the moon. The time of the reflection, long or short, proves the vastness of the dewdrop, and the vastness of the moon in the sky.

When the truth doesn't fill our body and mind, we think we have had enough. When the truth fills our body and mind, we realize that something is missing. For example, when we look at the ocean from a boat, with no land in sight, it seems circular and nothing else. But the ocean is neither round nor square, and its features are infinite in variety. It is like a palace. It is like a jewel. Only to our eyes, only for a moment, does it seem circular. All things are like this. Although there are numberless aspects to all things, we see only as far as our vision can reach. And in our vision of all things, we must appreciate that although they may look round or square, the other aspects of oceans or mountains are infinite in variety, and that universes lie all around us. It is like this everywhere, right here, in the tiniest drop of water.

When a fish swims, it swims on and on, and there is no end to the water. When a bird flies, it flies on and on, and there is no end to the sky. There was never a fish that swam out of the water, or a bird that flew out of the sky. When they need a little water or sky, they use just a little; when they need a lot, they use a lot. Thus, they use all of it at every moment, and in every place they have perfect freedom.

But if there were a bird that first wanted to examine the size of the sky, or a fish that first wanted to examine the extent of the water, and then try to fly or swim, it would never find its way. When we find where we are at this moment, then our everyday life is itself the manifestation of the truth. For the place, the way, is neither large nor small, neither self nor other. It has never existed before, and it is not coming into existence now. It is simply as it is.

Thus in our practice of Buddhism, when we master one truth, we master all truths; and when we complete one activity, we complete all activities. The place is here; the way leads everywhere. So understanding is not easy, because it is simultaneous with the complete attainment of the Buddha's teaching. Even though we have already attained supreme enlightenment, we may not realize it. Some may, and some may not.

One day, while Zen Master Pao-ch'e of Mount Ma-ku was fanning himself, a monk came up to him and said, "Master, the nature of the wind is permanent, and there is no place it doesn't reach. Why then do you need to fan yourself?"

"You understand that the nature of the wind is permanent," the Master said, "but you don't understand that it reaches everywhere."

"What does it mean that it reaches everywhere?" the monk said.

The Master just fanned himself.

The monk bowed with deep respect.

This is how Buddhism is experienced and correctly transmitted. Those who say that we shouldn't use a fan, because the wind is everywhere, understand neither permanence nor the nature of the wind. Because the nature of the wind is permanent, the wind of Buddhism brings forth the gold of the earth and turns its long rivers into wine.

———

THE PRACTICE OF MEDITATION

Truth is perfect and complete in itself. It is not something newly discovered; it has always existed.

Truth is not far away. It is nearer than near. There is no need to attain it, since not one of your steps leads away from it.

Don't follow the advice of others; rather, learn to listen to the voice within yourself. Your body and mind will become one, and you will realize the unity of all things.

Even the slightest movement of your conceptual thought will prevent you from entering the palace of wisdom.

The Buddha meditated for six years; Bodhidharma for nine. If such effort was required of these ancient Masters, how much more is required of you.

Your search among books, sifting and shuffling through other people's words, may lead you to the depths of knowledge, but it cannot help you to see the reflection of your true self. When you have thrown away all your conceptions of mind and body, the original person will appear, in his fullness.

To obtain the inestimable benefits of meditation, you should first make a firm decision to practice every day. Your meditation room should be clean and quiet. Wear loose clothing and remove your shoes. Sit on a cushion, with legs crossed, in as comfortable a manner as possible. Keep your back straight. Don't lean to the left or right; don't tip forward or bend back. Your ears should be in line with your shoulders. Keep your tongue at the roof of your mouth and close your lips. Your eyes should be slightly open, unfocused on the floor at a forty-five-degree angle. Breathe through your nostrils.

Before you begin meditation, take several slow, deep breaths. Hold your body erect, allowing your breathing to become normal again. Many thoughts will crowd into your mind. Don't dwell on thoughts of good or bad. Don't desire to attain enlightenment. Let your thoughts come and go, without getting involved in them or trying to suppress them. Think the unthinkable. In other words, think no-thinking.

Meditation is not a way to enlightenment, nor is it a method of achieving anything at all. It is peace and blessedness itself. It is the actualization of wisdom, the ultimate truth of the oneness of all things.

In your meditation, you yourself are the mirror reflecting the solution of your problems. The human mind has absolute freedom within its true nature. You can attain this freedom intuitively. Don't work toward freedom; but allow the work itself to be freedom.

When you want to rest, move your body slowly, and quietly

stand up. Practice this meditation in the morning or in the evening or at any leisure time during the day. You will soon realize that your mental burdens are dropping away one by one, and that you are gaining an intuitive power previously undreamed of.

There have been thousands upon thousands of people who have practiced meditation and obtained its fruits. Don't doubt its possibilities because of the simplicity of its method. If you can't find the truth right where you are, where else do you think you will find it?

Life is short, and no one knows what the next moment will bring. Cultivate your mind while you still have the opportunity. You will soon discover the treasure of wisdom, which in turn you can share abundantly with others, bringing them happiness and peace.

Rumi opens his lips and the praise pours out. Even the smallest leaf shines like a mirror. Nothing is simply itself. The price of metaphors plummets. The whole world becomes a love song. What's the opposite of the blues?

He sings of the lover, drunk with union. The Beloved is here, there, in, out. He has found a spring in the garden, gushing with red wine. But what about the plants? The real miracle: turning wine into water.

Little by little, wean yourself. This is the gist of what I have to say. From an embryo, whose nourishment comes in the blood, move to an infant drinking milk, to a child on solid food, to a searcher after wisdom, to a hunter of more invisible game.

Think how it is to have a conversation with an embryo. You might say, "The world outside is vast and intricate. There are wheatfields and mountain passes, and orchards in bloom. At night there are millions of galaxies, and in sunlight the beauty of friends dancing at a wedding."

You ask the embryo why he, or she, stays cooped up in the dark with eyes closed. Listen to the answer.

There is no "other world." I only know what I've experienced. You must be hallucinating.

———

A long cry at midnight near the mosque, a dying cry. The young man sitting there hears and thinks, "That sound doesn't make me afraid. Why should it? It's the drumbeat announcing a celebration! It means, we should start cooking the joy-soup!" He hears beyond his death-fear, to the Union. "It's time for that Merging in me now, or it's time to leave my body." He jumps up and shouts to God, *If you can be human, come inside me now!* The signal of a death-yell splits him open. Gold pours down, many kinds, from all directions, gold coins, liquid gold, gold cloth, gold bars. They pile up, almost blocking the doors of the mosque. The young man works all night carrying the gold away in sacks and burying it, and coming back for more. The timid church-members sleep through it all.

If you think I'm talking about actual gold, you're like those children who pretend that pieces of broken dishes are money, so that any time they see pottery shards, they think of money, as when you hear the word *gold* and think, "Goody."

This is the other gold, that glows in your chest when you love. The enchanted mosque is in *there*, and the pointed cry is a candle-flame on the altar. The young man is a moth who gambles himself and wins. A True Human Being is not human! This candle does not burn. It illuminates. Some candles burn themselves, and one another, up. Others taste like a surprise of roses in a room, and you just a stranger who wandered in.

———

A certain person came to the Friend's door and knocked.

"Who's there?"

"It's me."

The Friend answered, "Go away. There's no place for raw meat at this table."

The individual went wandering for a year. Nothing but the fire of separation can change hypocrisy and ego. The person returned completely cooked, walked up and down in front of the Friend's house, gently knocked.

"Who is it?"

"You."

"Please come in, my Self. There's no place in this house for two."

Translated by Coleman Barks with Reynold A. Nicholson

———

Moses heard a shepherd on the road praying, "God, where are You? I want to help You, to fix your shoes and comb Your hair. I want to wash Your clothes and pick the lice off. I want to bring You milk, to kiss Your little hands and feet when it's time for You to go to bed. I want to sweep Your room and keep it neat. God, my sheep and goats are Yours. All I can say, remembering You, is *ayyyy* and *ahhhhhhhhh*."

Moses could stand it no longer. "*Who* are you talking to?"

"The One who made us, and made the earth and made the sky."

"Don't talk about shoes and socks with God! And what's this with *Your little hands and feet*? Such blasphemous familiarity sounds like you're chatting with your uncles. Only something that grows needs milk. Only someone with feet needs shoes. Not God! Even if you meant God's human representatives, as when God said, 'I was sick, and you did not visit me,' even then this tone would be foolish and irreverent.

"Use appropriate terms. *Fatima* is a fine name for a woman, but if you call a man *Fatima*, it's an insult. Body-and-birth language are right for us on this side of the river, but not for addressing the Origin, not for Allah."

The shepherd repented and tore his clothes and sighed and wandered out into the desert. A sudden revelation came then to Moses. God's Voice: *You have separated Me from one of My own. Did you come as a Prophet to unite, or to sever? I have given each being a separate and unique way of seeing and knowing and saying that knowledge. What seems wrong to you is right for him. What is poison to one is honey to someone else. Purity and impurity, sloth and diligence in worship, these mean nothing to Me. I am apart from all that. Ways of worshiping are not to be ranked as better or worse than one another. Hindus do Hindu things. The Dravidian Muslims in India do what they do. It's all praise, it's all right. It's not Me that's glorified in acts of worship. It's the worshipers! I don't hear the words they say. I look inside at the humility. That broken-open lowliness is the Reality, not the language! Forget phraseology. I want burning,* burning. *Be Friends with your* burning. *Burn up your thinking and your forms of expression! Moses, those who pay attention to ways of behaving and speaking are one sort. Lovers who burn are another.*

Don't impose a property tax on a burned-out village. Don't scold the Lover. The "wrong" way he talks is better than a hundred "right" ways of others. Inside the Kaaba it doesn't matter which direction you point your prayer rug. The ocean diver doesn't need snowshoes. The Love-Religion has no code or doctrine. Only God. So the ruby has nothing engraved on it. It doesn't need markings.

God began speaking deeper mysteries to Moses. Vision and words, which cannot be recorded here, poured into and through him. He left himself and came back. He went to Eternity and came back here. Many times this happened. It's foolish of me to try and say this. If I did say it, it would uproot our human intelligences. It would shatter all writing pens.

Moses ran after the shepherd. He followed the bewildered footprints, in one place moving straight like a castle across a chessboard. In another, sideways, like a bishop. Now surging like a wave cresting, now sliding down like a fish, with always his feet making geomancy symbols in the sand, recording his wandering state.

Moses finally caught up with him. "I was wrong. God has revealed to me that there are no rules for worship. Say whatever and however your loving tells you to. Your sweet blasphemy is the truest devotion. Through you a whole world is freed. Loosen your tongue and don't worry what comes out. It's all the Light of the Spirit."

The shepherd replied, "Moses, Moses, I've gone beyond even that. You applied the whip, and my horse shied and jumped out of itself. The Divine Nature and my human nature came together. Bless your scolding hand and your arm. I can't say what happened. What I'm saying now is not my real condition. It can't be said." The shepherd grew quiet.

When you look in a mirror, you see yourself, not the state of the mirror. The fluteplayer puts breath into a flute, and who makes the music? Not the flute. The Fluteplayer! Whenever you speak praise or thanksgiving to God, it's always like this dear shepherd's simplicity. When you eventually see through the veils to how things really are, you will keep saying again and again, "This is certainly not the way we thought it was!"

Translated by Coleman Barks with John Moyne

———

Whoever is loved is beautiful, but the opposite is not true, that whoever is beautiful is loved. Real beauty is part of loved-ness, and that loved-ness is primary. If a being is loved, he or she has beauty, because a part cannot be separate from the whole. Many girls were more beautiful than Laila, but Majnun did not love them. "Let us bring some of these to meet you," they used to say to Majnun, and he would reply, "It's not the form of Laila that I love. Laila is not the form. You're looking at the cup, whereas I think only of the wine I drink from that cup. If you gave me a chalice studded with gemstones, but filled with vinegar or something other than wine, what use would that be? An old broken dipper-gourd with Laila-wine in it is better than a hundred precious goblets full of other liquid."

Passion is present when a man can distinguish between the wine and the container. Two men see a loaf of bread. One hasn't eaten anything for ten days. The other has eaten five times a day, every day. He sees the shape of the loaf. The other man with his urgent need sees *inside* into the taste, and into the nourishment the bread could give. Be that hungry, to see within all beings the Friend.

Creatures are cups. The sciences and the arts and all branches of knowledge are inscriptions around the outside of the cups. When a cup shatters, the writing can no longer be read. The wine's the thing! The wine that's held in the mold of these physical cups. Drink the wine and know what lasts and what to love. The man who truly asks must be sure of two things: One, that he's mistaken in what he's doing or thinking now. And two, that there is a wisdom he doesn't know yet. Asking is half of knowing.

Everyone turns toward someone. Look for one scarred by the King's polo stick.

A man or a woman is said to be absorbed when the water has total control of him, and he no control of the water. A swimmer moves around willfully. An absorbed being has no will but the water's going. Any word or act is not really personal, but the way the water has of speaking or doing. As when you hear a voice coming out of a wall, and you know that it's not the wall talking, but someone inside, or perhaps someone outside echoing off the wall. Saints are like that. They've achieved the condition of a wall, or a door.

Translated by Coleman Barks with A. J. Arberry

Impeccable.

Beati pauperes spiritu, quia ipsorum est regnum coelorum.
(Matthew 5:3)

Blessedness opened its mouth of wisdom and said: "Blessed are the poor in spirit, for theirs is the kingdom of heaven." All angels and all saints and all who were ever born must keep silent when the wisdom of the Father speaks; for all the wisdom of angels and created beings is a mere nothing before the bottomless wisdom of God. This wisdom has said that the poor are blessed.

Now there are two kinds of poverty. One is an outer poverty, and this is good and much to be praised in the man who takes it upon himself voluntarily, for the love of our Lord Jesus Christ, for he himself had it when he was on earth. About this poverty I will say nothing more now. But there is another poverty, an inner poverty, to which this saying of our Lord refers, when he says: "Blessed are the poor in spirit."

Now I beg you to be like this, so that you can understand this sermon; for I tell you in the eternal truth: If you are not like this truth which we are about to speak of, you cannot understand me.

Certain people have asked me what poverty is in itself, and what a poor man is. This is how we will answer.

Bishop Albert says that a poor man is one who cannot be satisfied by all things God ever created, and that is well said. But we will speak even better and take poverty in a higher sense: A poor man is one who wants nothing and knows nothing and has nothing. We will now speak about these three points, and I beg you, for the love of God, to understand this truth if you can; but if you can't understand it, don't worry, because the truth I am going to speak about is such that only a few good people will understand it.

First, we say that a poor man is one who wants nothing. There are some people who don't correctly understand what this means: these are the people who cling to their sense of self in penances and outer practices, which they think are very important. May God have mercy on them for knowing so little of divine truth! These people are called holy because of their outer appearance, but inside they are donkeys, for they can't recognize the divine truth. These people may say that a poor man is one who wants nothing; but they interpret it thus: a man should live in such a way that he never does his own will in anything but strives instead to do God's beloved will. These people do no wrong in this, for they mean well; and we praise them for that. May God grant them the kingdom of heaven in his mercy. But I say in the divine truth that they aren't poor men, or anything like poor men. They appear great only in the eyes of those who don't know any better. But I say that they are donkeys, who understand nothing of the divine truth. Perhaps they will gain the kingdom of heaven because of their good intentions; but of the poverty I will now speak about, they know nothing.

If someone were to ask me, what *is* a poor man who wants nothing, I would answer in this way: As long as a man still has it as his will to want to do God's beloved will, he doesn't have the poverty we are talking about; for this man has a will with which he wants to satisfy God's will, and that is not true poverty. For if a man is to be truly poor, he must be as empty of his created will as he was when he didn't exist. For I tell you by the eternal truth: as long as you have the will to do God's will, and the desire for eternity and for God, you are not truly poor. For only he is a poor man who wants nothing and desires nothing.

When I was in my first cause, I had no God, and I was cause of myself. I wanted nothing, I desired nothing, for I was an empty being and a knower of myself, rejoicing in the truth. I wanted myself and wanted no other thing; what I wanted I was, and what I was I wanted, and thus I was empty of God and of all things. But when I went out, by my own free will, and received my created being, then I had a God; for before there were creatures, God was not "God": he was what he was. But when creatures came to be and received their created being, then God was not "God" in himself, but he was "God" in the creatures.

Now we say that God, insofar as he is only "God," is not the ultimate goal of creatures. For the least of creatures *in* God has just as great a position. And if it were possible that a fly had intelligence and could with its mind search the eternal abyss of divine being out of which it came, we would have to say that God, with everything he is as "God," would be unable to fulfill or satisfy that fly. Therefore let us pray to God that we may be empty of "God," and that we may grasp the truth and eternally rejoice in it, there where the highest angels and the fly and the soul are equal, where I was pure being, and wanted what I was, and was what I wanted. So we say: if a man is to be poor in will, he must want and desire as little as he wanted and desired when he didn't exist. And this is the kind of poverty the man has who wants nothing.

Next, a poor man is one who knows nothing. We have sometimes said that a man should live in such a way that he doesn't live for himself or for the truth or for God. But now we will say it differently and say more: a man who is to have this poverty should live in such a way that he doesn't even know that he isn't living for himself or for the truth or for God; even more: he should be so empty of all knowing that he doesn't know or understand or feel that God lives in him; still more: he should be empty of all the understanding that lives in him. For when that man was in the eternal essence of God, nothing else lived in him; more: what lived there was himself. Therefore we say that a man should be as empty of his own knowing as he was when he didn't exist, and he should let God act as he wants, and he should be empty.

Everything that ever came from God is directed toward a pure activity. Man's proper activity is to love and to understand. Now the question is, what does blessedness most of all consist in? Certain masters have said that it consists in understanding, others say that it consists in loving, others say that it consists in understanding *and* in loving, and these speak better. But we say that it consists neither in understanding nor in loving; more: there is something in the soul from which both understanding and love flow; it itself doesn't understand or love as the powers of the soul do. Whoever understands this something, understands what blessedness consists in. This has neither before nor after, and it isn't waiting for anything to come, for it can neither gain nor lose. That is why it is deprived of the knowledge that God is acting in it; more: it is simply itself, rejoicing in itself as God does in himself. Therefore we say that a man should be so free and empty that he neither knows nor understands that God is acting in him. This is how a man can possess poverty.

The masters say that God is a being and an intelligent being and understands all things. But we say: God is neither a being nor intelligent, nor does he understand this or that. Thus God is empty of all things, and thus he *is* all things. Whoever is to be poor in spirit must be poor of all his own knowing, so that he knows nothing of God or of creatures or of himself. Thus it is necessary that a man desire to be unable to know and understand anything of the works of God. This is how a man can be poor of his own knowing.

Third, a poor man is one who has nothing. Many people have said that perfection is not having any of the material things of the earth, and that is quite true in one sense, if it is done voluntarily. But this is not the sense I am thinking of.

I said before that a poor man is one who doesn't even want to do God's will, but lives in such a way that he is as empty both of his own will and of God's will as he was when he didn't exist. Of this poverty we say that it is the highest poverty. Next we said that a poor man is one who knows nothing even of God's activity in him. When he is as empty of knowing and of understanding as God is empty of all things, that is the purest poverty. But the third kind of poverty, which I am going to speak about now, is the most intimate kind: this is when a man has nothing.

Now pay close attention to this! I have often said, and great masters say it too, that a man should be so empty of all things and of all activities, both inner and outer, that he can become a place for God, where God can act. Now we will say something else. If a man is empty of all creatures and of God and of himself, but if he is still such that God finds in him a place to act, then we say: as long as that is in the man, he isn't poor with the most intimate poverty. For in his works God doesn't intend that a man should have a place in himself where God can act; for poverty of spirit means that a man is so empty of God and of all his works that if God wants to act in the soul, he himself must be the place where he wants to act—and this he does gladly. For if he finds a man as poor as this, then God alone acts and the man allows God to act in him, and God is his own place of activity, because God is acting in himself. It is here, in this poverty, that a man attains the eternal essence which he once was and which he now is and which he will forever remain.

There is a saying of St. Paul's, where he says: "Everything I am, I am by the grace of God." Now this sermon seems to stand above grace and above being and above understanding and above will and above all desire—how then can St. Paul's words be true? The answer is that St. Paul's words are true in this way: it was necessary for God's grace to be in him, for God's grace made it possible in him that the accidental became essence. When grace finished and completed its work, Paul remained what he eternally was.

So we say that a man should be so poor that he neither is nor has in himself any place where God can act. Where a man keeps a place in himself, he keeps distinctions. Therefore I ask God to make me empty of God, for my essential being is above God, insofar as we conceive God as the source of all creatures. In that very being of God where God is above being and above distinctions, I was myself, I wanted myself and understood myself in order to make this man that I am. That is why I am my own cause according to my being, which is eternal, and not according to my becoming, which is temporal. And therefore I am unborn, and according to my unbornness I can never die. According to my unbornness, I have eternally existed and am now and will eternally remain. What I am according to my bornness will die and turn into nothing, for it is mortal; therefore it must in time be destroyed. In my birth all things were born, and I was cause of myself and of all things; and if I had willed it, I would not exist nor would anything exist; and if I didn't exist, "God" too would not exist. I am the cause that God is "God"; if I didn't exist, God would not be "God." But it isn't necessary to understand this.

A great master says that his return is nobler than his departure, and that is true. When I flowed out of God, all things said: God exists. But this can't make me blessed, for by this I understand that I am a creature. But when I break through and return where I am empty of my own will and of God's will and of all his works and of God himself, then I am above all creatures and am neither "God" nor creature; but I am what I was and what I will remain now and forever. Then I receive an impulse that will carry me above all the angels. In this impulse I receive such vast wealth that I can't be satisfied with God, as he is "God," or with all his divine works; for in this return, what I receive is that I and God are one. Then I am what I was, and then I neither increase nor decrease, for then I am an immovable cause that moves all things. Here, God finds no place in a man, for with this poverty the man achieves what he has eternally been and will forever remain. Here, God is one with the spirit, and that is the most intimate poverty that one can find.

Whoever doesn't understand this sermon shouldn't trouble his heart about it. For as long as a man isn't like this truth, he will not understand this sermon; for it is a naked truth that has come directly from God's heart.

May God help us to live in such a way that we experience it eternally. Amen.

———

The eye through which I see God is the same eye through which God sees me; my eye and God's eye are one eye, one seeing, one knowing, one love.

———

Christ's birth is always happening. And yet if it doesn't happen in me, how can it help me? Everything depends on that.

———

God *must* act and pour himself into you the moment he finds you ready. Don't imagine that God can be compared to an earthly carpenter, who acts or doesn't act, as he wishes; who can will to do something or leave it undone, according to his pleasure. It is *not* that way with God: where and when God finds you ready, he *must* act and overflow into you, just as when the air is clear and pure, the sun must overflow into it and cannot refrain from doing that.

———

Our bodily food is changed into us, but our spiritual food changes us into itself.

———

The Now in which God created the first man and the Now in which the last man will disappear and the Now in which I am speaking—all are the same in God, and there is only one Now.

———

Scripture says, "No one knows the Father but the Son." Therefore, if you want to know God, you must not only be like the Son, you must *be* the Son.

———

Many people imagine that there is "creaturely being" here and "divine being" in heaven. This is not true. You behold God in your life in the same perfection, and are blessed in exactly the same way, as in the afterlife.

———

All that is proper to the divine nature is also proper to the just and godly man; therefore such a man performs everything that God performs, and together with God he has created heaven and earth, and he is the begetter of the eternal Word, and without such a man God could do nothing.

———

You might ask, "How can I know if something is God's will?" My answer is, "If it were not God's will, it wouldn't exist even for an instant; so if something happens, it *must* be his will." If you truly enjoyed God's will, you would feel exactly as though you were in the kingdom of heaven, whatever happened to you or didn't happen to you.

———

God wants nothing of you but the gift of a peaceful heart.

Sheikh Maneri talks about four stages of faith in God. The first is merely verbal; the second is sincere; the third "is reached when a person's soul is illuminated in such a way that he is able to perceive every action flowing from a single source and deriving from a single agent." The fourth he describes in the following passage.

Sufi masters are of the opinion that, in the fourth stage, such a surfeit of the dazzling divine light becomes manifest to the pilgrim that every single particle that lies within his vision becomes concealed in the very luster of that light just as particles in the air are lost to sight on account of the brightness of the light emanating from the sun. This occurs not because the particles have ceased to exist but rather because the intensity of the sunlight makes it impossible that anything other than this concealment should result. In the same way, it is not true that a person becomes God—for God is infinitely greater than any man—nor has the person really ceased to exist, for ceasing to exist is one thing, and becoming lost to view quite another. "Before Your Unique Being, there is neither old nor new: everything is nothing, nothing at all. Yet He is what He is. How then can we remain separate from You?"

When "I" and "You" have passed away, God alone will remain.

When you look into a mirror, you do not see the mirror for the simple reason that your attention has become riveted on your own handsome reflection. You would not, however, go on to say that the mirror has ceased to exist, or that it has become beautiful, or that beauty has become a mirror. In a similar fashion, one can contemplate God's almighty power in the whole gamut of creation, without any distinction. Sufis describe this state as that of being entirely lost to oneself in contemplation of the Unique Being. "A person who attains such a blessed state says: 'His very brilliance blinds me to whatever descends.'"

Many have lost their balance here; for without the ever-present help of God's grace and favor, as well as the assistance of a spiritual guide, no one can traverse this wilderness. The guide should be a person who has passed through the ups and downs of the Way and tasted the unique sweetness of his all-demanding majesty, as well as the pleasure of his intoxicating beauty, and himself have attained enlightenment. This is the meaning of the following story. One day, Mansur al-Hallaj saw a famous Sufi, Ibrahim, wandering about in a wilderness. He inquired what he was about. "I am treading the path that leads to perfect trust in God," he replied. Mansur exclaimed, "If your whole life were to be passed in doing justice to this stage of trusting in God, then how would you ever reach that of being lost in divine contemplation?" It has been noted that fostering any sort of desire is really a waste of time, since it will just be a hindrance to contemplation.

Some people are admitted into the royal presence for an hour a week; others, for an hour or two a day; while yet others are absorbed in divine contemplation for the great part of their time. Beyond these four stages is one known as "losing consciousness of being lost in divine contemplation." This is due to the total absorption of the understanding of the pilgrim, which leads him to forget himself altogether, in the heightened awareness of the King who is unsurpassable in beauty and power. In an instant, the pilgrim is himself borne off to the concealment of nothingness. Everything slips away from him, for if he were to know anything else, then, in the opinion of the Sufis, it would be a sign of the distinction between seeing God apart from creation and seeing creation rooted in God. Hence we can understand how a person can lose sight of both himself and the entire creation in the dazzling light of God. The last vestige of self-awareness is itself lost in the rapture of this union.

"When you lose yourself in God, you proclaim the divine unity. Lose the sense of 'being lost'—that is complete detachment."

Hence it is that he forgets himself and the entire creation on account of this dazzling divine light. On account of this forgetfulness, all awareness of self is lost. There is no calling upon the name or observance of customs; awareness of whether one exists or not; explanation, allusion, or divine throne. In this world, all things pass away. There is no splendor except at this stage. Here, "everything perishes except His essence." Here alone is God actually seen face to face. Apart from here, one finds no trace of the Truth. "I am the Holy One." The absolutely unhampered realization of the Unique Being occurs only in this stage.

Translated by Paul Jackson, S.J.

The essence of prayer.

Lift up your heart to God with a meek stirring of love; and intend God himself and none of his created things. And be sure not to think of anything but himself, so that nothing may work in your mind or in your will but only himself. And do whatever you can to forget all the creatures that God ever made and all their works, so that your thought and your desire are not directed or stretched toward any of them, neither in general nor in particular. But let them be, and take no heed of them.

This is the work of the soul that most pleases God. All saints and angels rejoice in this work and hasten to help it with all their might. All men living on earth are wonderfully helped by this work, in ways that you cannot know. Even the souls in purgatory are eased of their pain by virtue of this work. You yourself are cleansed and made virtuous by no work so much as this. And yet it is the lightest work of all, and the soonest done, when a soul is helped with grace in palpable delight. But otherwise it is hard, and a miracle if you can do it.

Do not stop, therefore, but keep laboring in it till you feel delight. For when you first begin it, you find just a darkness and, as it were, a cloud of unknowing, you do not know what, except that you feel in your will a naked intent toward God. This darkness and this cloud, no matter what you do, is between you and your God, and hinders you, so that you can neither see him clearly by the light of understanding in your reason nor feel him in the sweetness of love in your affection. Therefore, prepare to abide in this darkness as long as you must, evermore crying after him whom you love. For if ever you are to see him or feel him in this life, it must always be in this cloud and in this darkness.

If you come to this cloud and dwell and work in it as I bid you, just as this cloud of unknowing is above you, between you and your God, so you must put a cloud of forgetting beneath you, between you and all the creatures that were ever made. You may think, perhaps, that you are very far from God, because this cloud of unknowing is between you and your God; but surely you are much farther from him when you have no cloud of forgetting between you and all the creatures that were ever made. Whenever I say "all the creatures that were ever made," I mean not only the creatures themselves, but also their works and conditions. I exclude no creatures, whether they be bodily creatures or spiritual; nor any condition or work of any creature, whether they be good or evil. But, to speak briefly, all should be hidden under the cloud of forgetting.

For although it is very profitable sometimes to think of certain conditions and deeds of certain special creatures, nevertheless in this work it profits little or nothing. Because remembrance or thinking of any creatures that God ever made, or of any of their deeds either, is a kind of spiritual light; for the eye of your soul is opened on it and fixed on it, as the eye of an archer is fixed on the spot he is shooting at. And one thing I tell you, that everything you think about is above you for this time, and between you and your God. And you are that much farther from God if anything is in your mind but only God.

Indeed—if it be courteous and seemly to say—in this work it profits little or nothing to think upon the kindness or the worthiness of God, or upon our Lady, or upon the saints or angels in heaven, or upon the joys of heaven: that is to say, with a special concentration upon them, as though you would by that concentration feed and increase your purpose. I believe that in no way would it do so in this work. For although it is good to think upon the kindness of God, and to love him and praise him for it: yet it is far better to think upon the naked being of him, and to love him and praise him for himself.

———

But now you ask me, "How shall I think upon God himself, and what is he?" To this I cannot answer you, except to say, "I don't know."

For with your question you have brought me into that same darkness and into that same cloud of unknowing that I want *you* to be in. For of all other creatures and their works—yes, and of the works of God himself—a man may through grace have fullness of knowing, and he can well think upon them; but upon God himself, no man can think. And therefore I wish to leave everything I can think, and choose for my love that thing which I cannot think. Because he may well be loved, but not thought. By love he may be gotten and held; but by thinking, never. And therefore, although it is good sometimes to think upon the kindness and the worthiness of God in particular, and although it is a joy and a proper part of contemplation, nevertheless in this work it shall be cast down and covered with a cloud of forgetting. And you shall step above it stalwartly, but eagerly, with a devout and a pleasing stirring of love, and try to pierce that darkness above you. And smite upon that thick cloud of unknowing with a sharp dart of longing love; and do not stop for anything that may happen.

———

Where another man would bid you to gather your powers and your senses wholly within yourself, and worship God there—although he speaks well and truly; yes, and no man trulier if he were well understood—yet for fear that you may understand his words wrongly and in a bodily way, I will not bid you to do this. But thus will I bid you. See that you are in no way within yourself. And (to speak briefly) I do not want you to be outside yourself, or above, or behind, or on one side, or on the other.

"Where then," you say, "shall I be? Nowhere, according to you!" Now truly you speak well; for that is where I would have you be. Because nowhere bodily is everywhere spiritually. Take good care, then, that your spiritual work be nowhere bodily; and then wherever that thing is, on which you are working in your mind, there you will surely be in spirit, as truly as your body is in the place where you are bodily. And although your bodily senses can find nothing there to feed themselves on, for they think that what you are doing is nothing, go on doing this nothing, as long as you are doing it for God's love. And do not stop, therefore, but work hard in that nothing with a watchful desire in your will to have God, whom no man may know. For I tell you truly that I would rather be nowhere bodily, wrestling with that blind nothing, than to be so great a lord that I might when I wanted be everywhere bodily, merrily playing with all this something as a lord with his own.

Let go of this everywhere and this something, in exchange for this nowhere and this nothing. Do not worry if your senses cannot understand this nothing, for this is why I love it much the better. It is so worthy a thing in itself that they cannot understand it. This nothing may better be felt than seen; for it is most blind and most dark to those who have for just a little while looked upon it. Nevertheless (to speak more truly) a soul is blinded in feeling it because of an abundance of spiritual light, rather than because of any darkness or lack of bodily light. Who is it that calls it nothing? Surely it is our outer man and not our inner. Our inner man calls it All; for it teaches him to understand all things bodily or spiritual, without any special knowledge of any one thing in itself.

Dame Julian has the distinction of being the earliest woman writer in English and the healthiest, most openhearted of Christian saints. She isn't officially a saint, but her book—indescribably sweet, tender, and whole—is a miracle far beyond the official miracles.

In her usual loving way, Dame Julian makes a crucial point here: that there are no accidents. God is not a well-intentioned bungler. All things that happen, even the most ostensibly terrible ones, happen by God's will. If you don't see the point, please look again. The point is a sharp one; you won't see it till you feel it, cutting out your mistaken ideas like a scalpel. There are no accidents. To realize this is to enter into God's love. It is a truth that should be placed on the doorposts of our houses and in our hearts.

At this same time our good Lord showed me a sight of his intimate love. I saw that he is to us everything that is good and comforting for our help. He is our clothing that, for love, wraps us and winds us about, embraces us and all-encloses us, for tender love, so that he can never leave us; being to us everything that is good, as I saw.

Also in this he showed me a little thing, the size of a hazelnut, lying in the palm of my hand, as it seemed to me; and it was as round as a ball. I looked upon it with the eye of my understanding, and thought, "What may this be?" And the answer was thus: "It is all that is made." I was amazed that it could last, for I thought it might suddenly fall into nothingness, it was so little. And I was answered in my understanding: "It lasts, and ever shall last, for God loves it; and even so everything has its being, by the love of God."

In this little thing I saw three properties. The first is that God made it, the second that God loves it, the third that God keeps it. And what did I see in this? Truly, the Maker, the Lover, and the Keeper. For till I am substantially oned to him, I can never have full rest nor true bliss; that is to say, till I am so fastened to him that there is no created thing between my God and me.

This little thing that is made: it seemed as though it would fall into nothingness, it was so little. We need to have knowledge of this and to naught everything that is made, so that we can love and have God who is unmade. For this is the reason why we are not all in ease of heart and soul: that we seek here rest in this thing that is so little and in which there is no rest, and we do not know our God who is all-mighty, all-wise, all-good. For he is true rest. It is God's will to be known, and it pleases him that we rest in him; for all that is beneath him is not sufficient for us. And this is the reason why no soul can rest till it is naughted of all things that are made. When it is willingly naughted, for love, so as to have him who is all, then it is able to receive spiritual rest.

And also our good Lord revealed that it is very greatly pleasing to him that a simple soul come to him nakedly and plainly and intimately. For this is the natural yearning of the soul, by the touching of the Holy Spirit, as I am given to understand by this revelation: *God, of your goodness, give me yourself; for you are enough to me, and I can ask nothing that is less that would be full worship of you; and if I ask anything that is less, I will always be lacking; but only in you do I have all.*

And these words are very lovely to the soul, and very near to touching the will of our Lord. For his goodness fills all his creatures and all his blessed works, and overflows without end. For he is the endlessness, and he made us only for himself, and restored us by his blessed passion, and ever keeps us in his blessed love; and all this is of his goodness.

———

The highest prayer is to the goodness of God, which comes down to us in the lowest part of our need. It created our soul and keeps it alive and makes it grow in grace and in virtue. It is nearest in nature and readiest in grace, for it is the same grace that the soul seeks and ever shall, till we truly know our God, who has enclosed us all in himself.

A man walks upright, and the food is closed in his body as if in a well-made purse. And when the time of his necessity comes, it is opened and shut again, in a most fitting manner. And that it is God who does this, is shown when he says he comes down to us to the lowest part of our need. For he does not despise what he made, nor does he disdain to serve us in the simplest function that belongs to our body naturally, for love of the soul that he made in his own likeness. For as the body is clad in the cloth, and the flesh in the skin, and the bones in the flesh, and the heart in the trunk, so are we, soul and body, clad and enclosed in the goodness of God. Yes, and more intimately, for all these vanish and waste away; but the goodness of God is ever whole and nearer to us, beyond any comparison. For truly our lover desires that the soul cleave to him with all its might, and that we may ever more cleave to his goodness. For of all things that the heart can think, this pleases God most and soonest profits the soul. For our soul is so preciously loved by him who is highest that this overpasses the knowing of all creatures. That is to say, there is no creature that can know how much and how sweetly and how tenderly our maker loves us. And therefore we can with his grace and his help continue in spiritual beholding, with everlasting wonder at this high, overpassing, unmeasurable love that our lord has for us in his goodness; and therefore we may with reverence ask of our lover all that we will, for our natural will is to have God, and the good will of God is to have us, and we can never cease willing or loving till we have him in fullness of joy.

———

And after this I saw God in a point, that is to say in my understanding, by which vision I saw that he is in all things. I beheld with care, seeing and knowing in that sight that he does all that is done. I marveled at that vision with a soft dread, and thought: What is sin? For I saw truly that God does all things, be they never so little. And I saw truly that nothing is done by chance or by accident, but all by the foreseeing wisdom of God. If it be chance or accident in the sight of man, our blindness and unforesight is the cause. For those things that are in the foreseeing wisdom of God from without beginning, which rightfully and worshipfully and continually he leads to the best end, as they come about fall to us suddenly, without our knowledge; and thus by our blindness and our unforesight we say that these things are by chance and accident.

Thus I understood in this revelation of love, for I well know that in the sight of our lord God there is no chance or accident; wherefore I had to grant that all things that are done are well done, for our lord God does all. For at this time the working of creatures was not revealed, but the working of our lord God in the creatures; for he is at the mid-point of all things, and he does all. And I was sure that he does no sin; and here I saw truly that sin is no deed, for in all this, sin was not revealed. And I did not wish to marvel at this, but beheld our lord, what he would reveal. And thus, as well as it could be at the time, the rightfulness of God's working was revealed to the soul. Rightfulness has two lovely properties: it is right and it is full. And so are all the works of our lord, and they lack no working of mercy or of grace, for they are all rightful, and nothing at all is absent in them.

This vision was revealed to my understanding, for our lord wants to have the soul truly turned to the beholding of him, and of all his works in general. For they are fully good, and all his judgments are easy and sweet, and bringing to great ease the soul that is turned from the beholding of the blind judgment of man to the lovely sweet judgment of our lord God. For man beholds some deeds as well done and some deeds as evil, but our lord beholds them not so, for as all that exists in nature is of God's making, so all that is done is rightly of God's doing. For it is easy to understand that the best deed is well done; and as well as the best and highest deed that is done, so well is the least deed done, and all things in the rightness and in the order that our lord ordained for it without beginning, for there is no doer but he.

I saw most truly that he never changed his purpose in any manner of thing, nor ever shall, without end. For there was nothing unknown to him in his rightful ordinance without beginning, and therefore all things were set in order, before anything was made, as it would exist without end. And no manner of thing will fail in that respect, for he has made all things fully good.

And therefore the blessed trinity is always fully pleased with all his works; and all this he revealed most blessedly, meaning thus: See, I am God. See, I am in all things. See, I do all things. See, I never remove my hands from my works, nor ever shall, without end. See, I lead all things to the end that I ordain them for, from without beginning, by the same might, wisdom, and love that I made them with; how should anything be amiss? Thus mightily, wisely, and lovingly was the soul examined in this vision. Then I saw truly that I had to assent, with great reverence and joy in God.

———

Prayer ones the soul to God, for though the soul is always like God in nature and in substance, it is often unlike him in condition, through sin on man's part. Then prayer is a witness that the soul wills as God wills, and it comforts the conscience and enables man for grace. And thus he teaches us to pray and mightily to trust that we shall have it; for he beholds us in love, and wants to make us partners in his good will and work. And therefore he moves us to pray for what it pleases him to do, and for this prayer and good will that we have by his gift he will reward us and give us endless treasure. And this was revealed in this saying: If you beseech it.

In this saying God showed such great pleasure and such great delight, as if he were much beholden to us for each good deed that we do; and yet it is he who does it. And therefore we beseech him mightily to do the thing that pleases him, as if he said: How could you please me more than to beseech me mightily, wisely, and earnestly the thing that I want to have done? And thus the soul by prayer is accorded with God.

But when our courteous lord by his special grace reveals himself to our soul, we have what we desire, and then we do not see, for that time, what more we should pray, but all our intent with all our might is wholly set to the beholding of him. And this is a high, unperceivable prayer, as I see it; for the whole cause wherefore we pray is to be oned into the vision and the beholding of him to whom we pray, marvelously rejoicing with reverent dread, and with such great sweetness and delight in him that we can pray nothing at all but as he moves us at the time.

———

This book is begun by God's gift and his grace, but it is not yet performed, as I see it. For charity, let us pray all together with God's working, thanking, trusting, rejoicing, for thus will our good lord be prayed, by the understanding that I took in all his own meaning, and in the sweet words where he says full merrily: I am the ground of your beseeching. For truly I saw and understood in our lord's meaning that he revealed it because he wants to have it known more than it is. In which knowing he wants to give us grace to love him and cleave to him, for he beholds his heavenly treasure with so great love on earth that he will give us more light and solace in heavenly joy, by drawing our hearts from the sorrow and darkness which we are in.

And from the time that it was revealed, I desired many times to know in what was our lord's meaning. And fifteen years after and more, I was answered in spiritual understanding, when he said: What, do you want to know your lord's meaning in this thing? Know it well, love was his meaning. Who reveals it to you? Love. What did he reveal to you? Love. Why does he reveal it to you? For love. Remain in this, and you shall know more of the same. But you shall never know different in this, without end.

Thus I was taught that love is our lord's meaning. And I saw most surely in this and in all, that before God made us he loved us, which love was never slaked nor ever shall be. And in this love he has done all his works, and in this love he has made all things profitable to us, and in this love our life is everlasting. In our creation we had beginning, but the love in which he made us was in him from without beginning. In this love we have our beginning, and all this shall we see in God without end.

Moving from the spiritual to the worldly is, when we enter Montaigne, a wonderfully bracing experience. As Zen Master Seung Sahn once wrote, "After so much suffering in Nirvanic castles, / what a joy to sink into this world!" Crawling among the cups and saucers, he sniffs toward the truth, baffled and fascinated, with a deep trust in Nature, and with complete honesty about himself, down to his slightest foibles. In what other writer is egotism so enchanting? His wisdom is earthy, political, humane, mellow, skeptical yet trusting, witty yet generous. And his personal motto, "Que sçais-je?" ("What do I know?"), hints at the primal question: "What am I?"

The following piece is the conclusion of "On Experience," the last essay in his book.

I, who boast of embracing the enjoyments of life so carefully and so particularly, find in them, when I look at them very keenly, little more than wind. But what of it? We are all wind. And even the wind, more wisely than we, loves to bluster and toss about and is content with its own functions, without desiring stability and solidity, qualities that do not belong to it.

The pure pleasures of the imagination, as well as the pains, some say, are the greatest, as was expressed by the scales of Critolaus. It is no wonder; it composes them to its own liking and cuts them out of whole cloth. Every day I see notable and, perhaps, desirable examples of this. But I, who am of a mixed and coarse make-up, cannot bite so fully at this single and simple object, but that I let myself go quite grossly after the present pleasures of the general human law, intellectually sensual, and sensually intellectual. The Cyrenaic philosophers hold that like bodily pains, so also bodily pleasures are more powerful, as being both double and more fit.

There are some who from savage stupidity, as Aristotle says, are disgusted with them; I know some who are so from ambition. Why don't they also give up breathing? Why don't they live on their own air and refuse light because it is free and costs them neither invention nor effort? Just to see, let Mars, or Pallas, or Mercury supply them with sustenance instead of Venus, Ceres, and Bacchus. Won't they try to square the circle while perched on their wives! I hate to have people tell us to keep our minds in the clouds while our bodies are at table. I would not have the mind nailed down to it nor wallowing at it, but paying attention to it; sitting at it, not lying down to it.

Aristippus defended the body alone, as if we had no soul; Zeno embraced only the soul, as if we had no body. In error, both of them. Pythagoras, they say, followed a philosophy that was all contemplation; Socrates, one that was all conduct and action; Plato found the balance between the two. But they say this to tell a good story, and the true balance is found in Socrates, and Plato is much more Socratic than Pythagorean, and it becomes him better.

When I dance, I dance; when I sleep, I sleep; yes, and when I walk alone in a beautiful orchard, if my thoughts have been concerned with extraneous incidents for some part of the time, for some other part I lead them back again to the walk, to the orchard, to the sweetness of this solitude, and to myself. Nature has in motherly fashion observed this principle, that the actions she has enjoined on us for our need should also give us pleasure; and she invites us to them not only through reason, but also through appetite. It is wrong to infringe her laws.

When I see both Caesar and Alexander, in the very thick of their great undertakings, so fully enjoying natural and, therefore, necessary and just pleasures, I do not say that this is relaxing their minds, I say that it is making them firmer, subjecting these violent occupations and laborious thoughts, by the vigor of their spirit, to the usage of everyday life. Wise men, if they had believed that the latter was their ordinary occupation, and the former the extraordinary.

We are great fools. "He has passed his life in idleness," we say. "I have done nothing today." What! haven't you lived? That is not only the fundamental but the most illustrious of your occupations. "Had I been put in a position to manage great affairs, I would have shown what I could do." Have you been able to think out and manage your life? You have performed the greatest work of all. In order to show and release her powers, Nature has no need of fortune; she shows herself equally on all levels, and behind a curtain as well as without one. To compose our character is our duty, not to compose books, and to win, not battles and provinces, but order and tranquility in our conduct. Our great and glorious masterpiece is to live appropriately. All other things, to rule, to lay up treasure, to build, are at most but little appendices and props.

I take pleasure in seeing an army general, at the foot of a breach he intends to attack presently, giving himself up wholly and freely to his dinner and to conversation with his friends; and Brutus, with heaven and earth conspiring against him and against Roman liberty, stealing some hour of the night from his rounds to read and annotate Polybius with full composure. It is for little souls, buried under the weight of business, not to be able to disengage themselves cleanly from it, or to lay it aside and take it up again.

Whether it be in jest or in earnest that the theological and Sorbonical wine has become proverbial, and their banquets too, I think it is right that they should dine all the more comfortably and pleasantly for having employed the morning profitably and seriously in the duties of their schools. The consciousness of having spent the other hours well is a proper and savory sauce for the dinner table. Thus did the sages live. And that inimitable striving after virtue which astonishes us in both of the Catos, that disposition, severe to the point of being troublesome, did thus submit gently and contentedly to the laws of human nature, and of Venus and Bacchus, in accordance with the precepts of their sect, which require the perfect sage to be an expert and versed in the use of natural pleasures as in any other duty of life.

Ease and affability do marvelous honor, it seems to me, and are most becoming to a strong and generous soul. Epaminondas did not think that to join in the dance of the boys of his city, to sing, to play an instrument, and to engage attentively in these things detracted at all from the honor of his glorious victories and the perfect purity of character that was his. And among so many admirable actions of Scipio, the grandfather, a person worthy to be reputed of a heavenly extraction, there is nothing that imparts more charm to him than to see him playing carelessly and childishly at picking up and selecting shells and running potato-races along the seashore with Laelius, and in bad weather amusing and tickling himself by writing comedies depicting the commonest and most vulgar actions of men; and, with his head full of that wonderful campaign against Hannibal and Africa, visiting the schools in Sicily, and attending lectures on philosophy to the point of arming to the teeth the blind envy of his enemies at Rome. Nor is there anything more remarkable in Socrates than that in his old age he finds time to take lessons in dancing and playing instruments, and thinks it time well spent.

This same man was once seen standing in a trance a whole day and night in the presence of all the Greek army, caught up and enraptured by some profound thought. He was seen, the first among so many valiant men of the army, to run to the relief of Alcibiades, who was overwhelmed by the enemy, to cover him with his body, and to free him from the press by sheer force of arms; and the first among all the people of Athens, outraged like him at so shameful a spectacle, to come forward to rescue Theramenes, whom the Thirty Tyrants were having led off to death by their satellites, and he desisted from this bold undertaking only at the remonstrance of Theramenes himself, though he was followed by only two men in all. He was seen, when courted by a beauty with whom he was in love, to maintain strict abstinence when necessary. He was seen, in the battle of Delium, to pick up and save Xenophon, who had been thrown from his horse. He was constantly seen to march to war and walk on ice barefoot, to wear the same gown in winter and in summer, to surpass all his companions in the endurance of toil, and to eat no differently at a feast than at an ordinary meal. He was seen for twenty-seven years to endure with the same countenance hunger, poverty, the indocility of his children, the claws of his wife; and in the end calumny, tyranny, imprisonment, fetters, and poison. But if that man was invited to a drinking bout by the duty of civility, he was also the one who was the best soldier in the army. And he never refused to play at nuts with the children, or to ride a hobby-horse with them, and he did it gracefully, for all actions, says philosophy, are equally becoming and honorable in a wise man. We have material enough, and we ought never to weary of presenting the image of this great man as a pattern and model of all kinds of perfection. There are very few examples of life that are full and pure, and those who educate us are unfair when they put before us every day weak and defective models, scarcely good in a single trait, which rather pull us backward, corrupters rather than correctors.

People are wrong: it is much easier to go along the sides where the far edge serves as a limit and a guide, than by the middle way, which is broad and open, and to go by art, than by nature; but it is also much less noble and commendable. Greatness of soul is not so much mounting high and pressing forward, as knowing how to put oneself in order and circumscribe oneself. It regards as great all that is enough and shows its elevation by preferring moderate things to eminent ones. There is nothing so beautiful and just as to play the man well and fitly, nor any knowledge so arduous as to know how to live this life well and naturally; and of all our maladies the most barbarous is to despise our being.

He who wants to set his soul apart, let him do it boldly, if he can, when the body is ill, to free it from the contagion; otherwise, on the contrary, let the soul assist and favor the body and not refuse to participate in its natural pleasures and take conjugal enjoyment in them, bringing to them moderation, if it is the wiser of the two, lest through lack of discretion they be confounded with pain. Intemperance is the plague of sensual pleasure; and temperance is not its scourge, it is its seasoning. Eudoxus, who set up pleasure as the sovereign good, and his fellows, who raised it to such a high value, savored it in its most charming sweetness by means of temperance, which they had in singular and exemplary degree.

I order my soul to look upon pain and pleasure with a gaze equally disciplined and equally firm, but gaily at the one, and severely at the other, and according to its ability, as anxious to extinguish the one as to extend the other. Viewing good things sanely involves viewing bad things sanely. And pain has something not to be avoided in its gentle beginning, and pleasure something to be avoided in its excessive ending. Plato couples them together and holds that it is equally the duty of fortitude to fight against pain and against the immoderate and seductive blandishments of pleasure. They are two fountains: whoever draws the proper amount from the proper one, at the proper time, whether city, man, or beast, he is very fortunate. The first must be taken as medicine and through necessity more sparingly; the other through thirst, but not to drunkenness. Pain, pleasure, love, hatred, are the first things that a child feels; if, when Reason comes, they attach themselves to her, that is virtue.

I have a vocabulary all my own. I "pass the time" when it is rainy and disagreeable; when the weather is good, I don't want to pass it; I savor it, I cling to it. We must hasten over the bad and settle upon the good. This ordinary phrase "pastime" and "passing the time" represents the practice of those wise folk who think they cannot make better use of their life than to let it flow away and to escape from it, to pass it away, and to dodge it, and, as far as in them lies, to ignore it and to run away from it as something tiresome and contemptible. But I know it to be otherwise and find it both agreeable and worthy to be prized, even in its last decline in which I now enjoy it; and Nature has placed it in our hands fitted out with such favorable conditions that we have only ourselves to blame if it burdens us and if it escapes from us unprofitably. Nevertheless, I am composing myself to lose it without regret, but as something that by its nature has to be lost, not as something annoying and troublesome. Moreover, not to dislike dying is appropriate only to those who like living. It requires management to enjoy it. I enjoy it twice as much as others, for the measure of enjoyment depends on the greater or lesser degree of attention that we give it. Especially at this moment when I perceive mine to be so brief in time, I try to increase it in weight; I try to arrest the rapidity of its flight by the rapidity with which I seize upon it, and by the vigor in using it to compensate for the haste of its ebb. The shorter my possession of life is, the deeper and fuller I must make it.

Others feel the sweetness of contentment and prosperity; I feel it as well as they, but it is not in passing and slipping by. Rather we must study it, savor it, and ruminate it in order to give due thanks for it to him who grants it to us. They enjoy the other pleasures as they do that of sleep, without being conscious of them. To the end that even sleep should not escape me thus stupidly, I once saw fit to have mine disturbed so that I might catch a glimpse of it. I meditate upon a pleasure, I don't skim over it; I sound it and bend my reason, now grown peevish and hard to please, to welcome it. Do I find myself in some state of tranquility? Is there some sensual pleasure that tickles me? I don't let my senses pilfer it, I make my soul join in it, not to bind herself to it, but to take pleasure in it, not to lose but to find herself in it. And I set her on her part to viewing herself in this prosperous estate, to weighing and appreciating and amplifying the happiness of it. She makes due reckoning of how much she stands indebted to God for being at peace with her conscience and free from inner passions, for having her body in its natural state, enjoying regularly and adequately the gentle and pleasing functions by which he of his grace is pleased to compensate the sufferings with which his justice chastises us in its turn; of how much it is worth to her to be lodged at such a point that wherever she casts her glance the sky is calm about her: no desire, no fear or doubt that troubles the air for her, no difficulty past, present, or future over which her imagination may not pass without hurt. This consideration takes on great luster by being compared with conditions different from mine. Thus I place before myself in a thousand aspects those who are carried away and tossed about by fortune or their own error, and also those nearer my bent who accept their good fortune so listlessly and indifferently. These are the people who really "pass their time"; they pass over the present and what they possess, to be the slaves of hope, and for the shadows and vain images which fancy dangles before them, which hasten and prolong their flight the more thay are pursued. The fruit and goal of their pursuit is to pursue, as Alexander said that the objective of his work was to work.

For my part, then, I love life and cultivate it, such as it has pleased God to bestow it upon us. I do not go about wishing that it might be free from the necessity of eating and drinking, and I should think I erred no less excusably to wish that the necessity might be doubled. Nor do I wish that we should sustain ourselves by merely putting into our mouth a little of that drug by which Epimenides took away his appetite and kept himself alive; nor that we should beget children insensibly with our fingers or heels, but rather, speaking with due reverence, that we might beget them voluptuously with our fingers and heels; nor that the body should be without desire and without titillation. Those are ungrateful and unfair complaints. I accept heartily and gratefully what Nature has done for me, and I am pleased with myself and proud of myself for it. We do wrong to that great and omnipotent Giver by refusing his gift, nullifying and disfiguring it. Being all good, he has made all things good.

Of philosophical opinions, I most readily embrace those that are most solid, that is to say, most human and most our own; my opinions, in keeping with my conduct, are low and humble. Philosophy is very childish, in my opinion, when she bristles up and preaches to us that it is a barbarous alliance to marry the divine with the earthly, the reasonable with the unreasonable, the severe with the indulgent, the honorable with the dishonorable; that sensual pleasure is a brutish thing unworthy of being enjoyed by a wise man; that the sole pleasure he derives from the enjoyment of a beautiful young wife is the pleasure of his consciousness in performing an action that is fitting, like putting on his boots for a useful ride. May her followers have no more right or sinews or sap in deflowering their wives than her lessons have!

This is not what Socrates, her teacher and ours, says. He prizes, as he ought, bodily pleasure, but he prefers that of the mind, as having more power, constancy, ease, variety, and dignity. The latter by no means goes alone, according to him (he is not so fantastic), but only comes first. For him temperance is the moderator, not the adversary, of pleasures.

Nature is a gentle guide, but no more gentle than wise and just. I seek her footprints everywhere. We have confused them with artificial tracks, and because of that the sovereign good of the Academics and the Peripatetics, which is "to live according to Nature," becomes hard to limit and express; as does that of the Stoics, a neighbor to the other, which is "to consent to Nature." Isn't it an error to consider some actions less worthy because they are necessary? So they will not knock it out of my head that the marriage of pleasure with necessity, with which, says an ancient, the gods always conspire, is a very fitting one. To what end do we dismember by divorce a structure composed of so close and brotherly a correspondence? On the contrary, let us bind it together again by mutual services. Let the mind rouse and quicken the heaviness of the body, and the body check and make fast the levity of the mind.

There is no part unworthy of our care in this gift that God has given us; we stand accountable for it even to a single hair. And it is not a perfunctory charge to man to direct man according to his nature; it is express, plain, and of prime importance, and the Creator has given it to us seriously and sternly.

Come now and see, have some man tell you someday the engrossing ideas and fancies that he gets into his head and for the sake of which he diverts his thoughts from a good meal and complains of the time he spends in feeding himself. You will find that there is nothing so insipid in all the dishes on your table as this fine entertainment of his mind (for the most part we would be better off to go to sleep completely than to keep awake for what we do stay awake for), and you will find that his ideas and his aims are not worth your stew. Though they were the raptures of Archimedes himself, what of it? I am not here referring to or mixing up with the childish rabble of men that we are, or with the vanity of the desires and thoughts that distract us, those venerable souls exalted by the ardor of devotion and religion to a constant and conscientious meditation on divine things, who, anticipating by force of a lively and vehement hope the enjoyment of eternal nourishment, the final goal and last step of Christian desires, the sole constant and incorruptible pleasure, disdain to apply themselves to our beggarly, fleeting, and ambiguous comforts, and readily resign to the body the care and enjoyment of sensual and temporal fodder. That is a privileged study. Between ourselves, these are things that I have always seen to be in remarkable agreement: supercelestial thoughts and subterranean conduct.

Aesop, that great man, saw his master pissing as he walked. "What next?" said he. "Must we shit as we run?" Let us manage our time, there will still remain a great deal that is idle and ill employed. Our mind likes to think it doesn't have enough leisure hours to do its own business unless it dissociates itself from the body for that little time when the body really needs it.

They want to get out of themselves and escape from humanity. That is folly: instead of transforming themselves into angels, they transform themselves into beasts; instead of raising, they lower themselves. These transcendental humors frighten me, like lofty and inaccessible places; and nothing is so hard for me to digest in the life of Socrates as his ecstasies and possessions by his daemon, nothing is so human in Plato as that for which they say he is called divine. And of our sciences, those seem to me the most terrestrial and low that have soared the highest. And I find nothing so humble and so mortal in the life of Alexander as his fancies about his immortalization. Philotas gave him a witty nip in his answer. He congratulated him by letter on the oracle of Jupiter Ammon which had placed him among the gods: "As far as you are concerned, I am very glad of it; but the men may well be pitied who will have to live with and obey a man who exceeds and is not concerned with a man's measure."

The nice inscription with which the Athenians honored the entry of Pompey into their city is in agreement with my meaning:

You are as much a deity
as you admit yourself a man.

It is an absolute perfection, and as it were divine, for a man to know how to rightfully enjoy his being. We seek other conditions because we don't understand the use of our own, and go out of ourselves because we don't know what it is like within. Yet it is no use for us to mount on stilts, for on stilts we must still walk with our own legs. And upon the loftiest throne in the world we are still sitting on our own ass.

The most beautiful lives, in my opinion, are those which conform to the common and human model, with order, but without miracle and without extravagant behavior. Now old age needs to be treated a little more tenderly. Let us commend it to that god who is the protector of health and wisdom, but a gay and sociable wisdom:

Grant me, Apollo, contentment with what I have
and let me enjoy, whole in mind and in body,
    an old age not lacking in honor
        and cheered by the presence of the poem.

Translated by Charles Cotton; revised by William Carey Hazlitt

Spinoza is one of the three greatest Jewish teachers, along with Jesus and the author of Job, *and the only one of the great Western philosophers who deserves to be compared to Lao-tzu or the Buddha. He lived with the irreproachable integrity of someone who understands not in his head but in his blood and bones.*

Spinoza defines the term "God" as "a being absolutely infinite—that is, a substance consisting of an infinity of attributes, each one of which expresses an eternal and infinite essence." In less precise words, he means "ultimate reality," or "the totality of all things that exist in time-space, in thought, and in all other inconceivable realms," or (as we might say today in America) "the Tao."

Sir and Very Welcome Friend,

Your letter of December 12th (enclosed in another letter of December 24th) didn't reach me until the 26th, while I was at Schiedam. I gathered from it that you have a great love for the truth, and that it alone is the aim of all your efforts. Since I too aim at nothing else, this made me decide not only to grant your request, as well as I can, by answering the questions you have sent me or will send me in the future, but also to do everything I can to further a closer acquaintance and a sincere friendship between us. Of all things beyond my power, I value nothing more than friendship with people who sincerely love the truth, for I believe that of the things beyond our power, there is nothing in the world we can love with tranquility except such people. Because the love such people feel for one another is founded on the love each one has for the truth, it is as impossible to disturb it as it is not to embrace the truth once it has been perceived. Moreover, it is the greatest and most satisfying source of happiness that we can find among things beyond our power, since nothing but the truth can unite different opinions and temperaments. I will not mention the great advantages that follow from it, because I don't want to detain you any longer with things you undoubtedly know already. I have said this much just to show you how glad I am to have this, and any future, opportunity of serving you.

To take advantage of the present opportunity, I will try to answer your question, which turns on the following point: that it seems to clearly follow from God's providence, which is identical with his will, as well as from God's cooperation and continuous creation of things, either that there are no such things as sins and evil, or that God is the cause of sins and evil. You do not, however, explain what you mean by "evil." As far as I can see from the example you give of Adam's determined will, by "evil" you seem to mean the will itself, insofar as it is conceived to be determined in such a way, or insofar as it is opposed to God's prohibition. Therefore you conclude (and I agree with you, if it were so) that it is absurd to adopt either alternative: either that God causes anything opposed to his will, or that what is opposed to God's will can be good. For myself, however, I cannot admit that sins and evil are something positive, much less that anything can exist or happen against God's will. On the contrary, not only do I assert that sin is not something positive, but I also maintain that only when we speak inaccurately, or in a human way, can we say that we sin against God, as in the expression that men anger God.

As to the first point, we know that everything that exists, considered in itself and without relation to anything else, involves perfection, which extends, in each thing, as far as the thing's essence does. For essence is nothing other than perfection. As an example, I too take Adam's decision, or determined will, to eat the forbidden fruit. This decision, or determined will, considered only in itself, involves as much perfection as it expresses essence. We can understand this from the fact that we can't conceive imperfection in things unless we consider them in relation to other things that have more essence.

Therefore we can't find any imperfection in Adam's decision if we consider it in itself and don't compare it with other things that are more perfect or show a more perfect state. Indeed, we can compare it with innumerable other things that are comparatively much more imperfect, such as stones, logs, etc. And in fact everyone admits this. For the same qualities that we regard with dislike and aversion in humans, we admire in animals—for example, the pugnacity of bees, the jealousy of doves, etc. We despise these qualities in humans but we consider animals more perfect because of them. Since this is true, it clearly follows that sins, because they indicate nothing but imperfection, cannot consist in anything that expresses essence, as Adam's decision or his carrying out of it do.

Furthermore, we can't say that Adam's will was opposed to God's will, and that it was evil because it was displeasing to God. For besides the fact that it would assume a great imperfection in God if anything happened against his will or if he wanted something he couldn't have, or if his nature were so limited that, like his creatures, he had sympathy with some things and antipathy for others—it would be completely opposed to the nature of God's will. For since God's will is identical with his understanding, it is as impossible for something to happen contrary to his will as it is for something to happen contrary to his understanding; in other words, anything that happened contrary to his will would have to be by nature contrary to his understanding, like a square circle. Therefore, since Adam's will or decision, considered in itself, was neither evil nor, properly speaking, contrary to God's will, it follows that God can be its cause, or rather, for the reason you indicated, he must be its cause; but not insofar as it was evil, for the evil in it was only a privation of a more perfect state, which Adam had to lose through that act. It is certain that privation is not something positive, and that the term is used only in relation to our understanding and not in relation to God's understanding. The difficulty arises because we give one and the same definition to all the singular things of the same kind (for example, all those who have the external shape of humans), and therefore we think that they are all equally capable of the highest perfection we can deduce from the definition. When we find someone whose acts are contrary to that perfection, we think that he is deprived of it, and that he deviates from his nature. We wouldn't do this if we hadn't brought him under such a definition and attributed such a nature to him. But since God doesn't know things abstractly and doesn't make general definitions of this kind, and since he doesn't attribute more essence to things than the divine understanding and power actually give them, it clearly follows that we can only speak of this privation in relation to our understanding, and not in relation to God's.

Thus, it seems to me, the difficulty is completely resolved. But in order to make the path smooth and to remove every objection, I will answer the two following questions: First, why does Scripture say that God wants the wicked to repent, and why did he forbid Adam to eat of the tree when he had ordained the opposite? Second, from what I have said it seems to follow that the wicked, by their pride, avarice, despair, etc., serve God no less than the good do by their generosity, patience, love, etc., because they too carry out God's will.

In answer to the first question, I say that Scripture, since it is primarily intended for the common people, continually speaks in human fashion. For the common people are not capable of understanding high matters. Therefore, I believe that all the things which God revealed to the prophets as being necessary for salvation are written in the form of laws. With this understanding, the prophets invented a whole parable. First, because God had revealed the means to salvation and destruction and was the cause of them, they described him as a king and lawgiver. The means, which are simply causes, they called laws and wrote them in the form of laws. Salvation and destruction, which are simply the effects that necessarily follow from these means, they represented as reward and punishment. And they arranged all their words more according to this parable than according to the truth. They constantly described God as a man, now angry, now merciful, now desiring what is future, now gripped by jealousy and suspicion, indeed even deceived by the devil. So philosophers and all who are above the law, that is, who follow virtue not in obedience to law, but from love, because it is the most excellent of all things, shouldn't be shocked by such words.

Thus the prohibition given to Adam consisted solely in this: God revealed to Adam that eating of the tree caused death; just as he reveals to us, through our natural intellect, that poison is deadly. If you ask what his purpose was in revealing this to him, I answer: to make him that much more perfect in knowledge. So to ask God why he didn't also give Adam a more perfect will is just as absurd as to ask why he didn't give the circle all the properties of a sphere.

As to the second difficulty, it is indeed true that the wicked carry out the will of God in their own fashion. But they aren't on that account to be compared to the good. For the more perfection something has, the more it participates in godliness, and the more it expresses God's perfection. Therefore, since the good have incalculably more perfection than the wicked, their virtue can't be compared with the virtue of the wicked, because the wicked lack the love of God, which comes from the knowledge of God, and by which alone we are, according to our human understanding, called the servants of God. Indeed, since they don't know God, the wicked are no more than a tool in the hand of the master, which serves unconsciously and is destroyed in the service. The good, on the other hand, serve consciously, and become more perfect by their service.

This, Sir, is all I can say now in answer to your question. I hope for nothing more than that it may satisfy you. But if you still find any difficulty, please let me know, so that I can try to remove it. For your part, you needn't hesitate, but as long as you aren't satisfied, I would like nothing better than to know your reasons, so that the truth may finally appear.

I wish I could write in the language in which I was brought up; perhaps I might express my thoughts better. Please excuse it, correct the mistakes yourself, and consider me

Your devoted friend and servant,

B. de Spinoza

———

From Book 2 of the *Ethics*

("On the Nature and Origin of the Mind")

It remains for me to point out the great advantages conferred by a knowledge of this doctrine [that in the human mind there is no absolute, or free, will]. We will easily realize this from the following considerations:

1. It teaches us that we act only from God's will, that we share in the divine nature, and that we share the more, the more perfect our actions are, and the more we understand God. This doctrine, therefore, besides giving us true peace of mind, also teaches us where our greatest happiness or blessedness lies: in the knowledge of God, by which we are led to do only those things that love and piety advise. From this we clearly understand how far astray from the true estimation of virtue are those who expect to be honored by God with the greatest rewards for their virtue and good deeds, as if these were the greatest servitude—as if virtue and the service of God were not happiness itself and the greatest freedom.

2. It teaches us how we should behave in relation to the things of fortune—those things which are not in our power, i.e., which do not follow from our own nature. For it shows us that we should expect and bear with equanimity both good and bad fortune, since all things follow from the eternal decree of God by the same necessity as it follows from the essence of a triangle that its three angles are equal to two right angles.

3. This doctrine contributes to our communal life in that it teaches us not to hate anyone, not to despise anyone, not to mock or envy or be angry with anyone; and also in that it teaches every

man to be content with what he has and to be helpful to his neighbor, not from weak-minded pity, partiality, or superstition, but by the guidance of reason alone, as time and circumstance require.

4. Finally, this doctrine also contributes considerably to the larger society, insofar as it teaches how citizens are to be governed and led, not so that they may become slaves, but so that they may freely do whatever things are best.

———

From Book 5 of the *Ethics*
("On Human Freedom")

Proposition 15: He who clearly and distinctly understands himself and his emotions loves God, and does so the more, the more he understands himself and his emotions.

Proposition 16: This love toward God must engage the mind more strongly than anything else.

Proposition 17: God is without passions, and is not affected by any emotion of pleasure or pain.

Proposition 19: He who loves God cannot endeavor that God should love him in return.

Proposition 20: This love toward God cannot be stained by the emotion of envy or jealousy: on the contrary, it is the more strengthened, the more people we imagine joined to God by the same bond of love.

Proposition 23: The human mind cannot be absolutely destroyed with the body, but something of it remains that is eternal.

Proposition 24: The more we understand particular things, the more we understand God.

Proposition 25: The highest endeavor of the mind, and its highest virtue, is to understand things by the third kind of knowledge [intuition: the kind of knowledge that "proceeds from an adequate idea of the absolute essence of certain attributes of God to the adequate knowledge of the essence of things"].

Proposition 27: From this third kind of knowledge arises the highest possible serenity of mind.

Proposition 30: Insofar as our mind knows itself and the body under the form of eternity, it necessarily has a knowledge of God, and knows that it is in God and is conceived through God.

Proposition 32: Whatever we understand by the third kind of knowledge, we take pleasure in, and our pleasure is accompanied by the idea of God as its cause.

Proposition 33: The intellectual love of God, which arises from the third kind of knowledge, is eternal.

Proposition 35: God loves himself with an infinite intellectual love.

Proposition 36: The mind's intellectual love of God is the very love of God by which God loves himself, not insofar as he is infinite, but insofar as he can be explained through the essence of the human mind, considered under the form of eternity; i.e., the mind's intellectual love of God is part of the infinite love with which God loves himself.

Proposition 42: Blessedness is not the reward of virtue, but is virtue itself; nor do we rejoice in it because we restrain our lusts, but, on the contrary, it is because we rejoice in it that we are able to restrain our lusts.

Note—I have thus completed everything that I wished to demonstrate concerning the mind's power over the emotions and the mind's freedom. From this it is apparent how powerful the wise man is, and how greatly he surpasses the ignorant man, who is driven only by his lusts. For not only is the ignorant man distracted in many ways by external causes and never able to enjoy true serenity of mind, but he also lives as if he were unaware of himself or God or things; and as soon as he ceases to be acted upon, he ceases to be.

The wise man, on the other hand, insofar as he is considered as such, is hardly ever troubled in spirit, but, being conscious of himself, and of God, and of things, by a certain eternal necessity, he never ceases to be, but always possesses true serenity of mind.

If the way I have pointed out as leading to this result seems exceedingly hard, it can nevertheless be found. It must indeed be hard, since it is found so seldom. For if true freedom were readily available and could be found without great effort, how is it possible that it should be neglected by almost everyone? But all things excellent are as difficult as they are rare.

The following pieces are like orchestral transcriptions of Psalm 8:

> When I look up at your heavens,
>   the work of your fingers,
>   the moon and the multitude of stars,
> what is man, that you love him,
>   and woman, that you gladden her heart?
> You have made them higher than any god
>   and have crowned them with glory and honor.

I love the richness, the thinginess and exhilaration of Traherne's language. He is a true innocent. It would be as much fun to take a walk with him as it would be to play catch with Ryōkan, or to fingerpaint with Blake.

You never enjoy the world aright till you see how a sand exhibits the wisdom and power of God; and prize in every thing the service which they do you by manifesting His glory and goodness to your soul, far more than the visible beauty on their surface or the material services they can do your body. Wine by its moisture quenches my thirst, whether I consider it or no; but to see it flowing from His love who gave it unto man, quenches the thirst even of the holy angels. To consider it is to drink it spiritually. To rejoice in its diffusion is to be of a public mind. And to take pleasure in all the benefits it does to all is heavenly, for so they do in heaven. To do so is to be divine and good, and to imitate our infinite and eternal Father.

Your enjoyment of the world is never right till every morning you awake in heaven; see yourself in your Father's palace; and look upon the skies and the earth and the air as celestial joys: having such a reverend esteem of all, as if you were among the angels. The bride of a monarch, in her husband's chamber, has no such causes of delight as you.

You never enjoy the world aright till the sea itself flows in your veins, till you are clothed with the heavens, and crowned with the stars; and perceive yourself to be the sole heir of the whole world; and more than so, because men are in it who are every one sole heirs, as well as you. Till you can sing and rejoice and delight in God, as misers do in gold, and kings in scepters, you never enjoy the world.

Till your spirit fills the whole world, and the stars are your jewels; till you are as familiar with the ways of God in all ages as with your walk and table; till you are intimately acquainted with that shady nothing out of which the world was made; till you love men so as to desire their happiness, with a thirst equal to the zeal of your own; till you delight in God for being good to all: you never enjoy the world. Till you more feel it than your private estate, and are more present in the hemisphere, considering the glories and the beauties there, than in your own house. Till you remember how lately you were made, and how wonderful it was when you came into it; and more rejoice in the palace of your glory, than if it had been made but today morning.

You never enjoy the world aright till you see all things in it so perfectly yours that you cannot desire them any other way; and till you are convinced that all things serve you best in their proper places. For can you desire to enjoy anything a better way than in God's image?

Your enjoyment is never right till you esteem every soul so great a treasure as our Savior does; and that the laws of God are sweeter than the honey and honeycomb because they command you to love them all in such perfect manner. For how are they God's treasures? Are they not the riches of His love? Is it not His goodness that makes Him glorious to them? Can the sun or stars serve Him any other way than by serving them? And how will you be the Son of God but by having a great soul like unto your Father's? The laws of God command you to live in His image: and to do so is to live in heaven.

Certainly Adam in Paradise had not more sweet and curious apprehensions of the world than I when I was a child. All appeared new, and strange at the first, inexpressibly rare, and delightful, and beautiful. I was a little stranger, which at my entrance into the world was saluted and surrounded with innumerable joys. My knowledge was divine. I knew by intuition those things which since my apostasy I collected again, by the highest reason. My very ignorance was advantageous. I seemed as one brought into the estate of innocence. All things were spotless and pure and glorious: yea, and infinitely mine, and joyful and precious. I knew not that there were any sins, or complaints, or laws. I dreamed not of poverties, contentions or vices. All tears and quarrels were hidden from my eyes. Everything was at rest, free, and immortal. I knew nothing of sickness or death, or exaction, in the absence of these I was entertained like an angel with the works of God in their splendor and glory; I saw all in the peace of Eden; heaven and earth did sing my Creator's praises, and could not make more melody to Adam than to me. All time was eternity, and a perpetual sabbath. Is it not strange that an infant should be heir of the world, and see those mysteries which the books of the learned never unfold?

The corn was orient and immortal wheat, which never should be reaped, nor was ever sown. I thought it had stood from everlasting to everlasting. The dust and stones of the street were as precious as gold. The gates were at first the end of the world, the green trees when I saw them first through one of the gates transported and ravished me; their sweetness and unusual beauty made my heart to leap, and almost mad with ecstasy, they were such strange and wonderful things. The men! O what venerable and reverend creatures did the aged seem! Immortal cherubims! And young men glittering and sparkling angels, and maids strange seraphic pieces of life and beauty! Boys and girls tumbling in the street, and playing, were moving jewels. I knew not that they were born or should die. But all things abided eternally as they were in their proper places. Eternity was manifest in the light of the day, and something infinite behind everything appeared: which talked with my expectation and moved my desire. The city seemed to stand in Eden, or to be built in heaven. The streets were mine, the temple was mine, the people were mine, their clothes and gold and silver were mine, as much as their sparkling eyes, fair skins and ruddy faces. The skies were mine, and so were the sun and moon and stars, and all the world was mine, and I the only spectator and enjoyer of it. I knew no churlish properties, nor bounds nor divisions: but all properties and divisions were mine: all treasures and the possessors of them. So that with much ado I was corrupted; and made to learn the dirty devices of this world. Which now I unlearn, and become as it were a little child again, that I may enter into the kingdom of God.

Before the first word: silence. Before the first light: light.

When you gaze at an object, you bring blessing to it. For through contemplation, you know that it is absolutely nothing without the divinity that permeates it. By means of this awareness, you draw greater vitality to that object from the divine source of life, since you bind that thing to absolute nothingness, the origin of all. On the other hand, if you look at that object as a separate thing, by your look that thing is cut off from its divine root and vitality.

Translated by Daniel C. Matt

———

I will teach you the best way to say Torah. You must be nothing but an ear that hears what the universe of the word is constantly saying within you. The moment you begin to hear what you yourself are saying, you must stop.

———

The creation of heaven and earth is the unfolding of something out of nothing, the descent from above to below. But the masters who in their work disengage themselves from what is bodily and do nothing but meditate on God, actually see the universe as it was in the state of nothingness before creation. They change the something back into the nothing. This is more miraculous: to begin from the lower state. As it is said in the Talmud: "Greater than the first miracle is the last."

Translated by Martin Buber, and Olga Marx

How do we deal with the wicked—the torturer, the rapist, the terrorist, the child-molester—and with the hatred and greed in ourselves? We need both justice and compassion, the right and the left eye of vision: only with the two can we see in depth. The twentieth-century Jewish mystic Rav Kook said, "It is our right to hate an evil man for his actions, but because his deepest self is the image of God, it is our duty to honor him with love."

A disciple asked Rabbi Shmelke, "We are commanded to love our neighbor as ourself. How can I do this if my neighbor has wronged me?"

The rabbi answered, "You must understand these words correctly. Love your neighbor like something which you yourself are. For all souls are one. Each is a spark from the original soul, and this soul is wholly inherent in all souls, just as your soul is in all members of your body. It may happen that your hand makes a mistake and hits you. But would you then take a stick and punish your hand because it lacked understanding, and so increase your pain? It is the same if your neighbor, who is of one soul with you, wrongs you because he does not understand. If you punish him, you only hurt yourself."

The disciple asked, "But if I see a man who is wicked before God, how can I love him?"

Rabbi Shmelke said, "Don't you know that the original soul came out of the essence of God, and that every human soul is a part of God? And will you have no mercy on Him, when you see that one of His holy sparks has been lost in a maze, and is almost stifled?"

Translated by Martin Buber, and Olga Marx

Choose anything, but follow it to the source.

The purpose of the creation of the world was the delight that God would receive from it, the great pleasure he would receive from emanating the souls of Israel, which would come down through many thousands and tens of thousands of worlds until they reached this world, where they would take a material shape and from which, from a great distance, they would purify themselves in order to approach him and cleave to him in their thoughts and in their love. And they would consider themselves to be nothing, for they would understand that without the power of God, who created them and who keeps them in existence, they are nothing, just as before the creation; and so there is nothing in the world but the Creator, blessed be he. This is the opposite of what people imagine: when they are not attached to God but to earthly things, they think that they exist, and they are great in their own eyes. And how can they be great, when one night they exist and the next night they die? Their days are like passing shadows, and even in their lives they are vanity. Thus, if they think that they exist, they certainly do not. But if, out of love for God, they think that they are nothing, and cleave to him with all their mental powers, they are very great, since the branch has come to the root and is one with the root. The root is the Infinite, therefore the branch is also infinite. It has lost its own existence, like a drop that has fallen into the great sea and is one with the waters of the sea and cannot be recognized as a separate thing.

Translated by Joseph Weiss

The circumstances of this speech, given in 1805, are as follows: A young Christian minister, representing a narrowhearted, bigoted Christianity, had been sent by the Evangelical Missionary Society of Massachusetts to open a center among the Senecas, and had said, among other things:

> *There is only one religion, and only one way to serve God, and if you do not embrace the right way you cannot be happy hereafter. You have never worshiped the Great Spirit in a manner acceptable to him; but have all your lives been in great errors and darkness.*

After two hours' consultation with the Seneca council of chiefs, Sa-Go-Ye-Wat-Ha gave his speech—a marvel of honesty, resoluteness, compassion, poignance, courtesy, wit, forensic skill, devastating innocence, and the religion of the forefathers: a religion that Jesus would have approved with all his heart.

According to the eyewitness account, after Sa-Go-Ye-Wat-Ha finished speaking, the Indians moved toward the missionary "to extend the parting hand of friendship; but the missionary said that he could not shake their hands, 'since there is no fellowship between the religion of God and the devil.' Thereupon the Indians smiled, and left."

SPEECH TO A CHRISTIAN MISSIONARY

Friend and Brother: It was the will of the Great Spirit that we should meet today. He directs all things, and he has given us a fine day for our council. He has taken his garment from before the sun and has caused the bright circle to shine upon us. Our eyes are opened so that we see clearly. Our ears are unstopped so that we have clearly heard the words you have spoken. For all these favors we thank the Great Spirit and him only.

Brother: This council fire was kindled by you. It was at your request that we came together. We have listened with attention to what you have said. You have asked us to speak our minds freely.

This gives us great joy, for we can now stand upright before you and can speak what we think. We have all heard your voice and we all speak to you as one man.

You say that you want an answer to your speech before you leave this place. It is right that you should have one, since you are a great distance from home, and we do not wish to detain you. But we will first look back a little, and tell you what our fathers have told us, and what we have heard from the white people.

Brother: Listen to what we say. There was a time when our fore-fathers owned this great continent. Their seats extended from the rising to the setting of the sun. The Great Spirit made it for the use of the red man. He created the buffalo, the deer, and other animals for food. He made the bear and the deer, and their skins served us for clothing. He scattered them over the country and taught us how to take them. He caused the earth to produce corn for bread. All this he did for his red children, because he loved them. If we had any disputes about hunting grounds, they were settled without spill-ing much blood. But an evil day came upon us. Your forefathers crossed the great waters and landed on this continent. Their num-bers were small. They found friends and not enemies. They told us they had fled from wicked men in their own country and had come here to enjoy their religion. They asked for a small seat. We had compassion for them and granted their request, and they sat down among us. We gave them corn and meat; they gave us poison* in re-turn. Tidings were carried back and more white people came among us. Yet we were not afraid of them. We saw them as friends. They called us brothers. We believed them and gave them a large seat. At length their numbers greatly increased. They wanted more land. They wanted our country. Our eyes were opened, and our minds became uneasy. Wars took place. Red men were paid to fight against red men, and many of our people were killed. They also

*Rum.

159

brought strong liquor among us. It was very strong and has killed thousands.

Brother: Our seats were once large, and yours were very small. You have now become a great people, and we hardly have a place left to spread our blankets. You have our country, but you are not yet satisfied. Now you want to force your religion on us.

Brother: Continue to listen. You say that you have been sent to teach us how to worship the Great Spirit agreeably to his mind, and that if we do not take hold of the religion which you white people teach we will be unhappy hereafter. You say that you are right and that we are lost. How do you know that this is true? We understand that your religion is written in a book. If it was meant for us as well as for you, why hasn't the Great Spirit given it to us? And not only to us, but why didn't he allow our forefathers to know that book, with the means of understanding it rightly? We know only what you tell us about it. How can we know when to believe, since we have been lied to so often by the white people?

You say there is only one way to worship and serve the Great Spirit. If there is only one religion, why do you white people differ so much about it? Why don't you all agree, since you can all read the book?

We do not understand these things. We are told that your religion was given to your forefathers and has been handed down, father to son. We also have a religion which was given to our forefathers and has been handed down to us, their children. We worship in that way. It teaches us to be grateful for all the favors we receive, to love one another, and to be united. We never quarrel about religion. We know that the Great Spirit is pleased that we follow the traditions of our forefathers, for in doing so we receive his blessing. He has given us abundance, and strength and vigor for the hunt. When we are hungry, the forest is filled with game; when we are thirsty, we drink at his pure streams; when we are tired, the leaves are our bed. We go to sleep content, and we wake up with gratitude to the Great Spirit. With renewed strength in our limbs, and bounding joy in our hearts, we feel blessed.

Brother: The Great Spirit has made us all. But he has made a great difference between his white and his red children. He has given us a different skin color and different customs. He has given great powers to you; about these he has not opened our eyes. We know that these things are true. Since he has made so great a difference between us in other things, why shouldn't we conclude that he has given us a different religion, according to our understanding? The Great Spirit does right. He knows what is best for his children. We are satisfied.

We do not worship the Great Spirit as the white men do, but we believe that forms of worship do not matter to the Great Spirit; what pleases him is the offering of a sincere heart, and this is how we worship him. We do not want to destroy your religion or to take it from you. We only want to enjoy our own.

Brother: We are told that you have been preaching to the white people in this place. These people are our neighbors. We are acquainted with them. We will wait a little while, and see what effect your preaching has on them. If we find that it does them good and makes them honest and less disposed to cheat the red man, we will consider again what you have said.

Brother: You have heard our answer to your talk, and this is all we have to say now. Since we are going to part, we will come and take you by the hand, and hope that the Great Spirit will protect you on your journey and return you safe to your friends.

For eighteen centuries we had been rooting for god against the devil, not realizing that each is a reflection of the divine. Imagining a hell makes heaven into a bore among the clouds, an everlasting Sunday service in starched clothes. Poor devil. Take away his horns and cackle, and there is the pure animal energy of a child. Of such is the kingdom of heaven.

Blake is the great prophet for our age. His insight about the body is a truth that not even Jesus, not even the Buddha, taught. At the marriage of heaven and hell, God is best man.

From *The Marriage of Heaven and Hell*

Without Contraries is no progression. Attraction and Repulsion, Reason and Energy, Love and Hate, are necessary to Human existence.

From these contraries spring what the religious call Good & Evil. Good is the passive that obeys Reason. Evil is the active springing from Energy.

Good is Heaven. Evil is Hell.

THE VOICE OF THE DEVIL

All Bibles or sacred codes have been the causes of the following Errors:

1. That Man has two real existing principles: Viz: a Body & a Soul.

2. That Energy, call'd Evil, is alone from the Body, & that Reason, call'd Good, is alone from the Soul.

3. That God will torment Man in Eternity for following his Energies.

But the following Contraries to these are True:

1. Man has no Body distinct from his Soul; for that call'd Body

is a portion of Soul discern'd by the five Senses, the chief inlets of Soul in this age.

2. Energy is the only life and is from the Body and Reason is the bound or outward circumference of Energy.

3. Energy is Eternal Delight.

Those who restrain desire, do so because theirs is weak enough to be restrained; and the restrainer or Reason usurps its place & governs the unwilling.

And being restrain'd, it by degrees becomes passive, till it is only the shadow of desire.

The history of this is written in Paradise Lost, & the Governor or Reason is call'd Messiah.

And the original Archangel, or possessor of the command of the heavenly host, is call'd the Devil or Satan, and his children are call'd Sin & Death.

But in the Book of Job, Milton's Messiah is call'd Satan.

For this history has been adopted by both parties.

It indeed appear'd to Reason as if Desire was cast out, but the Devil's account is, that the Messiah fell, & formed a heaven of what he stole from the Abyss.

This is shewn in the Gospel, where he prays to the Father to send the comforter, or Desire, that Reason may have Ideas to build on, the Jehovah of the Bible being no other than he who dwells in flaming fire.

Know that after Christ's death, he became Jehovah.

But in Milton, the Father is Destiny, the Son a Ratio of the five senses, & the Holy-ghost Vacuum!

Note: The reason Milton wrote in fetters when he wrote of Angels & God, and at liberty when of Devils & Hell, is because he was a true Poet and of the Devil's party without knowing it.

As I was walking among the fires of hell, delighted with the enjoyments of Genius, which to Angels look like torment and insanity, I collected some of their Proverbs; thinking that as the sayings used in a nation mark its character, so the Proverbs of Hell shew the nature of Infernal wisdom better than any description of buildings or garments.

When I came home: on the abyss of the five senses, where a flat sided steep frowns over the present world, I saw a mighty Devil folded in black clouds, hovering on the sides of the rock, with corroding fires he wrote the following sentence now percieved by the minds of men, & read by them on earth:

How do you know but ev'ry Bird that cuts the airy way,
Is an immense world of delight, clos'd by your senses five?

PROVERBS OF HELL

In seed time learn, in harvest teach, in winter enjoy.
Drive your cart and your plow over the bones of the dead.
The road of excess leads to the palace of wisdom.
Prudence is a rich ugly old maid courted by Incapacity.
He who desires but acts not, breeds pestilence.
The cut worm forgives the plow.
Dip him in the river who loves water.
A fool sees not the same tree that a wise man sees.
He whose face gives no light, shall never become a star.
Eternity is in love with the productions of time.
The busy bee has no time for sorrow.
The hours of folly are measur'd by the clock; but of wisdom, no
        clock can measure.
All wholesome food is caught without a net or a trap.
Bring out number, weight & measure in a year of dearth.
No bird soars too high, if he soars with his own wings.
A dead body revenges not injuries.

The most sublime act is to set another before you.

If the fool would persist in his folly he would become wise.

Folly is the cloke of knavery.

Shame is Pride's cloke.

Prisons are built with stones of Law, Brothels with bricks of
Religion.

The pride of the peacock is the glory of God.

The lust of the goat is the bounty of God.

The wrath of the lion is the wisdom of God.

The nakedness of woman is the work of God.

Excess of sorrow laughs. Excess of joy weeps.

The roaring of lions, the howling of wolves, the raging of the
stormy sea, and the destructive sword, are portions of
eternity, too great for the eye of man.

The fox condemns the trap, not himself.

Joys impregnate. Sorrows bring forth.

Let man wear the fell of the lion, woman the fleece of the sheep.

The bird a nest, the spider a web, man friendship.

The selfish smiling fool, & the sullen frowning fool shall be both
thought wise, that they may be a rod.

What is now proved was once only imagin'd.

The rat, the mouse, the fox, the rabbet watch the roots; the lion,
the tyger, the horse, the elephant, watch the fruits.

The cistern contains: the fountain overflows.

One thought fills immensity.

Always be ready to speak your mind, and a base man will avoid
you.

Every thing possible to be believ'd is an image of truth.

The eagle never lost so much time, as when he submitted to learn
of the crow.

The fox provides for himself, but God provides for the lion.

Think in the morning. Act in the noon. Eat in the evening. Sleep in
the night.

He who has suffer'd you to impose on him knows you.

As the plow follows words, so God rewards prayers.

The tygers of wrath are wiser than the horses of instruction.

Expect poison from the standing water.

You never know what is enough unless you know what is more
than enough.

Listen to the fool's reproach! it is a kingly title!

The eyes of fire, the nostrils of air, the mouth of water, the beard of
earth.

The weak in courage is strong in cunning.

The apple tree never asks the beech how he shall grow; nor the
lion, the horse, how he shall take his prey.

The thankful reciever bears a plentiful harvest.

If others had not been foolish, we should be so.

The soul of sweet delight can never be defil'd.

When thou seest an Eagle, thou seest a portion of Genius; lift up
thy head!

As the catterpiller chooses the fairest leaves to lay her eggs on, so
the priest lays his curse on the fairest joys.

To create a little flower is the labour of ages.

Damn braces. Bless relaxes.

The best wine is the oldest, the best water the newest.

Prayers plow not! Praises reap not!

Joys laugh not! Sorrows weep not!

The head Sublime, the heart Pathos, the genitals Beauty, the hands
& feet Proportion.

As the air to a bird or the sea to a fish, so is contempt to the
contemptible.

The crow wish'd every thing was black, the owl that every thing
was white.

Exuberance is Beauty.

If the lion was advised by the fox, he would be cunning.

Improvement makes straight roads; but the crooked roads
    without Improvement are roads of Genius.
Sooner murder an infant in its cradle than nurse unacted desires.
Where man is not, nature is barren.
Truth can never be told so as to be understood, and not be
    believ'd.

Enough! or Too much.

The ancient Poets animated all sensible objects with Gods or Ge-
niuses, calling them by the names and adorning them with the properties of woods, rivers, mountains, lakes, cities, nations, and whatever their enlarged & numerous senses could percieve.

And particularly they studied the genius of each city & country,
placing it under its mental deity;

Till a system was formed, which some took advantage of, & en-
slav'd the vulgar by attempting to realize or abstract the mental deities from their objects: thus began Priesthood;

Choosing forms of worship from poetic tales.

And at length they pronounc'd that the Gods had order'd such
things.

Thus men forgot that All deities reside in the human breast.

A MEMORABLE FANCY

The Prophets Isaiah and Ezekiel dined with me, and I asked them
how they dared so roundly to assert that God spoke to them; and
whether they did not think at the time that they would be misun-
derstood, & so be the cause of imposition.

Isaiah answer'd: "I saw no God, nor heard any, in a finite organ-
ical perception; but my senses discover'd the infinite in every thing,
and as I was then perswaded, & remain confirm'd, that the voice of
honest indignation is the voice of God, I cared not for conse-
quences, but wrote."

Then I asked: "does a firm perswasion that a thing is so, make it so?"

He replied: "All poets believe that it does, & in ages of imagination this firm perswasion removed mountains; but many are not capable of a firm perswasion of any thing."

Then Ezekiel said: "The philosophy of the east taught the first principles of human perception: some nations held one principle for the origin, & some another: we of Israel taught that the Poetic Genius (as you now call it) was the first principle and all the others merely derivative, which was the cause of our despising the Priests & Philosophers of other countries, and prophecying that all Gods would at last be proved to originate in ours & to be tributaries of the Poetic Genius; it was this that our great poet King David desired so fervently & invokes so pathetic'ly, saying by this he conquers enemies & governs kingdoms; and we so loved our God, that we cursed in his name all the deities of surrounding nations, and asserted that they had rebelled; from these opinions the vulgar came to think that all nations would at last be subject to the jews."

"This," said he, "like all firm perswasions, is come to pass; for all nations believe the jews' code and worship the jews' god, and what greater subjection can be?"

I heard this with some wonder, & must confess my own conviction. After dinner I ask'd Isaiah to favour the world with his lost works; he said none of equal value was lost. Ezekiel said the same of his.

I also asked Isaiah what made him go naked and barefoot three years? he answer'd: "the same that made our friend Diogenes, the Grecian."

I then asked Ezekiel why he ate dung, & lay so long on his right & left side? he answer'd: "the desire of raising other men into a perception of the infinite: this the North American tribes practise, & is he honest who resists his genius or conscience only for the sake of present ease or gratification?"

The ancient tradition that the world will be consumed in fire at the end of six thousand years is true, as I have heard from Hell.

For the cherub with his flaming sword is hereby commanded to leave his guard at the tree of life; and when he does, the whole creation will be consumed and appear infinite and holy, whereas it now appears finite & corrupt.

This will come to pass by an improvement of sensual enjoyment.

But first the notion that man has a body distinct from his soul is to be expunged; this I shall do by printing in the infernal method, by corrosives, which in Hell are salutary and medicinal, melting apparent surfaces away, and displaying the infinite which was hid.

If the doors of perception were cleansed every thing would appear to man as it is: infinite.

For man has closed himself up, till he sees all things thro' narrow chinks of his cavern.

The Giants who formed this world into its sensual existence and now seem to live in it in chains, are in truth the causes of its life & the sources of all activity; but the chains are the cunning of weak and tame minds which have power to resist energy; according to the proverb, the weak in courage is strong in cunning.

Thus one portion of being is the Prolific, the other the Devouring: to the devourer it seems as if the producer was in his chains; but it is not so, he only takes portions of existence and fancies that the whole.

But the Prolific would cease to be Prolific unless the Devourer, as a sea, recieved the excess of his delights.

Some will say: "Is not God alone the Prolific?" I answer: "God only Acts & Is, in existing beings or Men."

These two classes of men are always upon earth, & they should be enemies: whoever tries to reconcile them seeks to destroy existence.

Religion is an endeavor to reconcile the two.

Note: Jesus Christ did not wish to unite, but to separate them, as in the Parable of sheep and goats! & he says: "I came not to send Peace, but a Sword."

Messiah or Satan or Tempter was formerly thought to be one of the Antediluvians who are our Energies.

A MEMORABLE FANCY

Once I saw a Devil in a flame of fire, who arose before an Angel that sat on a cloud, and the Devil utter'd these words:

"The worship of God is: Honouring his gifts in other men, each according to his genius, and loving the greatest men best: those who envy or calumniate great men hate God; for there is no other God."

The Angel hearing this became almost blue, but mastering himself he grew yellow, & at last white, pink, & smiling, and then replied:

"Thou Idolater, is not God One? & is not he visible in Jesus Christ? and has not Jesus Christ given his sanction to the law of ten commandments, and are not all other men fools, sinners, & nothings?"

The Devil answer'd: "bray a fool in a morter with wheat, yet shall not his folly be beaten out of him; if Jesus Christ is the greatest man, you ought to love him in the greatest degree; now hear how he has given his sanction to the law of ten commandments: did he not mock at the sabbath, and so mock the sabbath's God? murder those who were murder'd because of him? turn away the law from the woman taken in adultery? steal the labor of others to support him? bear false witness when he omitted making a defence before Pilate? covet when he pray'd for his disciples, and when he bid them shake off the dust of their feet against such as refused to lodge them? I tell you, no virtue can exist without breaking these ten commandments. Jesus was all virtue, and acted from impulse, not from rules."

When he had so spoken, I beheld the Angel, who stretched out his arms, embracing the flame of fire, & he was consumed and arose as Elijah.

Note: This Angel, who is now become a Devil, is my particular friend; we often read the Bible together in its infernal or diabolical sense, which the world shall have if they behave well.

I have also The Bible of Hell, which the world shall have whether they will or no.

CHORUS

Let the priests of the Raven of Dawn, no longer in deadly black, with hoarse note curse the sons of joy. Nor his accepted brethren, whom, tyrant, he calls free, lay the bound or build the roof. Nor pale religious letchery call that virginity that wishes but acts not!

For every thing that lives is Holy.

"The holy and ardent Novalis," Emerson called him. He was a scientist by trade, a pure romantic by nature. "The more poetic," he wrote, "the more real. This is the core of my philosophy."

We are close to waking up when we dream that we are dreaming.

———

Philosophy is really homesickness.

———

We are alone with everything we love.

———

There is only *one* temple in the world and that is the human body.

———

Marriage is the highest mystery.

———

When you understand how to love *one* thing—then you also understand how best to love everything.

When gray comes, a mirror reflects gray; in sad times, even enlightened words are sad. Although Chief Seattle's vision did not penetrate to the depths, his love for the earth and his magnanimity are deeply moving. Can any decent white American read this speech without great shame?

SPEECH TO GOVERNOR STEVENS

Brothers: The sky above us has pitied our fathers for many hundreds of years. To us it looks unchanging, but it may change. Today it is fair. Tomorrow it may be covered with cloud.

My words are like the stars. They do not set. What Seattle says, the great chief Washington can count on as surely as our white brothers can count on the return of the seasons.

The White Chief's son says that his father sends us words of friendship and goodwill. This is kind of him, since we know he has little need of our friendship in return. His people are many, like the grass that covers the plains. My people are few, like the trees scattered by the storms on the grasslands.

The great—and good, I believe—White Chief sends us word that he wants to buy our land. But he will reserve us enough so that we can live comfortably. This seems generous, since the red man no longer has rights he need respect. It may also be wise, since we no longer need a large country. Once my people covered this land like a flood-tide moving with the wind across the shell-littered flats. But that time is gone, and with it the greatness of tribes now almost forgotten.

But I will not mourn the passing of my people. Nor do I blame our white brothers for causing it. We too were perhaps partly to blame. When our young men grow angry at some wrong, real or imagined, they make their faces ugly with black paint. Then their hearts are ugly and black. They are hard and their cruelty knows no limits. And our old men cannot restrain them.

Let us hope that the wars between the red man and his white brothers will never come again. We would have everything to lose and nothing to gain. Young men view revenge as gain, even when they lose their own lives. But the old men who stay behind in time of war, mothers with sons to lose—they know better.

Our great father Washington—for he must be our father now as well as yours, since King George has moved his boundary northward—our great and good father sends us word by his son, who is surely a great chief among his people, that he will protect us if we do what he wants. His brave soldiers will be a strong wall for my people, and his great warships will fill our harbors. Then our ancient enemies to the north—the Haidas and Tsimshians—will no longer frighten our women and old men. Then he will be our father and we will be his children.

But how can that ever be? Your God loves your people and hates mine. He puts his strong arm around the white man and leads him by the hand, as a father leads his little boy. He has abandoned his red children. He makes your people stronger every day. Soon they will flood all the land. But my people are an ebb tide, we will never return. No, the white man's God cannot love his red children or he would protect them. Now we are orphans. There is no one to help us.

So how can we be brothers? How can your father be our father, and make us prosper and send us dreams of future greatness? Your God is prejudiced. He came to the white man. We never saw him, never even heard his voice. He gave the white man laws, but he had no word for his red children whose numbers once filled this land as the stars filled the sky.

No, we are two separate races, and we must stay separate. There is little in common between us.

To us the ashes of our fathers are sacred. Their graves are holy ground. But you are wanderers, you leave your fathers' graves behind you, and you do not care.

Your religion was written on tables of stone by the iron finger of an angry God, so you would not forget it. The red man could never understand it or remember it. Our religion is the ways of the fore-fathers, the dreams of our old men, sent them by the Great Spirit, and the visions of our sachems. And it is written in the hearts of our people.

Your dead forget you and the country of their birth as soon as they go beyond the grave and walk among the stars. They are quickly forgotten and they never return. Our dead never forget this beautiful earth. It is their mother. They always love and remember her rivers, her great mountains, her valleys. They long for the living, who are lonely too and who long for the dead. And their spirits often return to visit and console us.

No, day and night cannot live together.

The red man has always retreated before the advancing white man, as the mist on the mountain slopes runs before the morning sun.

So your offer seems fair, and I think my people will accept it and go to the reservation you offer them. We will live apart, and in peace. For the words of the Great White Chief are like the words of nature speaking to my people out of great darkness—a darkness that gathers around us like the night fog moving inland from the sea.

It matters little where we spend the rest of our days. They are not many. The Indian's night will be dark. No bright star shines on his horizons. The wind is sad. Fate hunts the red man down. Wherever he goes, he will hear the approaching steps of his destroyer, and prepare to die, like the wounded doe who hears the steps of the hunter.

A few more moons, a few more winters, and none of the children of the great tribes that once lived in this wide earth or that roam now in small bands in the woods will be left to mourn the graves of a people once as powerful and as hopeful as yours.

But why should I mourn the passing of my people? Tribes are made of men, nothing more. Men come and go, like the waves of the sea. A tear, a prayer to the Great Spirit, a dirge, and they are gone from our longing eyes forever. Even the white man, whose God walked and talked with him as friend with friend, cannot be exempt from the common destiny.

We may be brothers after all. We shall see.

We will consider your offer. When we have decided, we will let you know. Should we accept, I here and now make this condition: we will never be denied the right to visit, at any time, the graves of our fathers and our friends.

Every part of this earth is sacred to my people. Every hillside, every valley, every clearing and wood, is holy in the memory and experience of my people. Even those unspeaking stones along the shore are loud with events and memories in the life of my people. The ground beneath your feet responds more lovingly to our steps than yours, because it is the ashes of our grandfathers. Our bare feet know the kindred touch. The earth is rich with the lives of our kin.

The young men, the mothers and girls, the little children who once lived and were happy here, still love these lonely places. And at evening the forests are dark with the presence of the dead. When the last red man has vanished from this earth, and his memory is only a story among the whites, these shores will still swarm with the invisible dead of my people. And when your children's children think they are alone in the fields, the forests, the shops, the highways, or the quiet of the woods, they will not be alone. There is no place in this country where a man can be alone. At night when the streets of your towns and cities are quiet, and you think they are empty, they will throng with the returning spirits that once thronged them, and that still love these places. The white man will never be alone.

So let him be just and deal kindly with my people. The dead have power too.

Adapted by William Arrowsmith

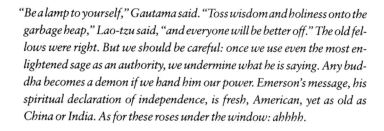

"Be a lamp to yourself," Gautama said. "Toss wisdom and holiness onto the garbage heap," Lao-tzu said, "and everyone will be better off." The old fellows were right. But we should be careful: once we use even the most enlightened sage as an authority, we undermine what he is saying. Any buddha becomes a demon if we hand him our power. Emerson's message, his spiritual declaration of independence, is fresh, American, yet as old as China or India. As for these roses under the window: ahhhh.

Whenever a mind is simple and receives a divine wisdom, old things pass away,—means, teachers, texts, temples fall; it lives now, and absorbs past and future into the present hour. All things are made sacred by relation to it,—one as much as another. All things are dissolved to their center by their cause, and in the universal miracle petty and particular miracles disappear. If therefore a man claims to know and speak of God and carries you backward to the phraseology of some old mouldered nation in another country, in another world, believe him not. Is the acorn better than the oak which is its fullness and completion? Is the parent better than the child into whom he has cast his ripened being? Whence then this worship of the past? The centuries are conspirators against the sanity and authority of the soul. Time and space are but physiological colors which the eye makes, but the soul is light: where it is, is day; where it was, is night; and history is an impertinence and an injury if it be anything more than a cheerful apologue or parable of my being and becoming.

Man is timid and apologetic; he is no longer upright; he dares not say "I think," "I am," but quotes some saint or sage. He is ashamed before the blade of grass or the blowing rose. These roses under my window make no reference to former roses or to better ones; they are for what they are; they exist with God today. There is no time to them. There is simply the rose; it is perfect in every moment of its existence. Before a leaf-bud has burst, its whole life acts; in the full-blown flower there is no more; in the leafless root there is no less. Its nature is satisfied and it satisfies nature in all moments alike. But man postpones or remembers; he does not live in the present, but with reverted eye laments the past, or, heedless of the riches that surround him, stands on tiptoe to foresee the future. He cannot be happy and strong until he too lives with nature in the present, above time.

———

Every thing in nature contains all the powers of nature. Every thing is made of one hidden stuff; as the naturalist sees one type under every metamorphosis, and regards a horse as a running man, a fish as a swimming man, a bird as a flying man, a tree as a rooted man. Each new form repeats not only the main character of the type, but part for part all the details, all the aims, furtherances, hindrances, energies, and whole system of every other. Every occupation, trade, art, transaction, is a compend of the world and a correlative of every other. Each one is an entire emblem of human life; of its good and ill, its trials, its enemies, its course and its end. And each one must somehow accommodate the whole man and recite all his destiny.

The world globes itself in a drop of dew. The microscope cannot find the animalcule which is less perfect for being little. Eyes, ears, taste, smell, motion, resistance, appetite, and organs of reproduction that take hold on eternity,—all find room to consist in the small creature. So do we put our life into every act. The true doctrine of omnipresence is that God reappears with all his parts in every moss and cobweb. The value of the universe contrives to throw itself into every point. If the good is there, so is the evil; if the affinity, so the repulsion; if the force, so the limitation.

Thus is the universe alive. All things are moral. That soul which within us is a sentiment, outside of us is a law. We feel its inspiration; out there in history we can see its fatal strength. "It is in the world, and the world was made by it." Justice is not postponed. A perfect equity adjusts its balance in all parts of life. The dice of God are always loaded. The world looks like a multiplication-table, or a mathematical equation, which, turn it how you will, balances itself. Take what figure you will, its exact value, nor more nor less, still returns to you. Every secret is told, every crime is punished, every virtue rewarded, every wrong redressed, in silence and certainty. What we call retribution is the universal necessity by which the whole appears wherever a part appears. If you see smoke, there must be fire. If you see a hand or a limb, you know that the trunk to which it belongs is there behind.

Every act rewards itself, or in other words integrates itself, in a twofold manner; first in the thing, or in real nature; and secondly in the circumstance, or in apparent nature. Men call the circumstance the retribution. The causal retribution is in the thing and is seen by the soul. The retribution in the circumstance is seen by the understanding; it is inseparable from the thing, but is often spread over a long time and so does not become distinct until after many years. The specific stripes may follow late after the offense, but they follow because they accompany it. Crime and punishment grow out of one stem. Punishment is a fruit that unsuspected ripens within the flower of the pleasure which concealed it. Cause and effect, means and ends, seed and fruit, cannot be severed; for the effect already blooms in the cause, the end preëxists in the means, the fruit in the seed.

———

Inevitably the universe wears our color, and every object falls successively into the subject itself. The subject exists, the subject enlarges; all things sooner or later fall into place. As I am, so I see; use what language we will, we can never say anything but what we are; Hermes, Cadmus, Columbus, Newton, Bonaparte, are the mind's ministers. Instead of feeling a poverty when we encounter a great man, let us treat the new comer like a travelling geologist who passes through our estate and shows us good slate, or limestone, or anthracite, in our brush pasture. The partial action of each strong mind in one direction is a telescope for the objects on which it is pointed. But every other part of knowledge is to be pushed to the same extravagance, ere the soul attains her due sphericity. Do you see that kitten chasing so prettily her own tail? If you could look with her eyes you might see her surrounded with hundreds of figures performing complex dramas, with tragic and comic issues, long conversations, many characters, many ups and downs of fate,—and meantime it is only puss and her tail. How long before our masquerade will end its noise of tambourines, laughter, and shouting, and we shall find it was a solitary performance? A subject and an object,—it takes so much to make the galvanic circuit complete, but magnitude adds nothing. What imports it whether it is Kepler and the sphere, Columbus and America, a reader and his book, or puss with her tail?

———

We lie in the lap of immense intelligence, which makes us receivers of its truth and organs of its activity.

———

Jove nods to Jove from behind each of us.

———

Every man's condition is a solution in hieroglyph to those inquiries he would put. He acts it as life before he apprehends it as truth.

———

The Sphinx must solve her own riddle.

How much more down-to-earth can you get than Thoreau's Yankee practicality? Yet with him, as with all honest people, the practical flows into the moral, and action is the mirror of contemplation. How dead-central his writings on civil disobedience and on wilderness have been for our age! We are lucky to have him as an ancestor.

Shams and delusions are esteemed for soundest truths, while reality is fabulous. If men would steadily observe realities only, and not allow themselves to be deluded, life, to compare it with such things as we know, would be like a fairy tale and the Arabian Nights' Entertainments. If we respected only what is inevitable and has a right to be, music and poetry would resound along the streets. When we are unhurried and wise, we perceive that only great and worthy things have any permanent and absolute existence, that petty fears and petty pleasures are but the shadow of the reality. This is always exhilarating and sublime. By closing the eyes and slumbering, and consenting to be deceived by shows, men establish and confirm their daily life of routine and habit everywhere, which still is built on purely illusory foundations. Children, who play life, discern its true law and relations more clearly than men, who fail to live it worthily, but who think they are wiser by experience, that is, by failure. I have read in a Hindoo book, that "there was a king's son, who, being expelled in infancy from his native city, was brought up by a forester, and, growing up to maturity in that state, imagined himself to belong to the barbarous race with which he lived. One of his father's ministers having discovered him, revealed to him what he was, and the misconception of his character was removed, and he knew himself to be a prince. So soul," continues the Hindoo philosopher, "from the circumstances in which it is placed, mistakes its own character, until the truth is revealed to it by some holy teacher, and then it knows itself to be *Brahme*." I perceive that we inhabitants of New England live this mean life that we do because our vision does not penetrate the surface of things. We think that that *is* which *appears* to be. If a man should walk through this town and see only the reality, where, think you, would the "Mill-dam" go to? If he should give us an account of the realities he beheld there, we should not recognize the place in his description. Look at a meeting-house, or a court-house, or a jail, or a shop, or a dwelling-house, and say what thing really is before a true gaze, and they would all go to pieces in your account of them. Men esteem truth remote, in the outskirts of the system, behind the farthest star, before Adam and after the last man. In eternity there is indeed something true and sublime. But all these times and places and occasions are now and here. God himself culminates in the present moment, and will never be more divine in the lapse of all the ages. And we are enabled to apprehend at all what is sublime and noble only by the perpetual instilling and drenching of the reality that surrounds us. The universe constantly and obediently answers to our conceptions; whether we travel fast or slow, the track is laid for us.

Does it seem contradictory that the greatest poets have the greatest trust in silence? But how can we truly love the world unless we love its beginning and end? As Rilke once wrote:

> We say release, and radiance, and roses,
> and echo upon everything that's known;
> and yet, behind the world our names enclose is
> the nameless: our true archetype and home.

AN EXPERIENCE

It could have been little more than a year ago that, in the castle garden which sloped down quite steeply to the sea, something strange happened to him. Walking back and forth with a book, as was his custom, he had happened to recline into the more or less shoulder-high fork of a shrublike tree, and in this position he immediately felt himself so pleasurably supported and so deeply soothed that he remained as he was, without reading, completely absorbed into Nature, in a nearly unconscious contemplation. Little by little his attention awakened to a feeling he had never known before: it was as if almost unnoticeable pulsations were passing into him from the inside of the tree; he explained this to himself quite easily by supposing that an otherwise invisible wind, perhaps blowing down the slope close to the ground, was making itself felt in the wood, though he had to acknowledge that the trunk seemed too thick to be moved so forcibly by such a mild breeze. What concerned him, however, was not to pass any kind of judgment; rather, he was more and more surprised, indeed astonished, by the effect of this pulsation which kept ceaselessly passing over into him; it seemed to him that he had never been filled by more delicate movements; his body was being treated, so to speak, like a soul, and made capable of absorbing a degree of influence which, in the usual distinctness of physical conditions, wouldn't really have been sensed at all. Nor could he correctly determine, during the first few moments, which of his senses it was through which he was receiving so delicate and extended a communication; moreover, the condition it had created in him was so perfect and continuous, different from all others, but so impossible to describe by the intensification of anything experienced before, that for all its exquisiteness he couldn't think of calling it a pleasure. Nevertheless, concerned as he always was to account for precisely the subtlest impressions, he asked himself insistently what was happening to him, and almost immediately found an expression that satisfied him as he said it aloud: he had passed over to the other side of Nature. As happens sometimes in a dream, this phrase now gave him joy, and he considered it almost completely apt. Everywhere and more and more regularly filled with this impulse which kept recurring in strangely interior intervals, his body became indescribably touching to him and of no further use than to be purely and cautiously present in, just as a ghost, already dwelling elsewhere, sadly enters what was tenderly laid aside, in order to belong once again, even if inattentively, to this once so indispensable world. Slowly looking around himself, without otherwise shifting his position, he recognized everything, remembered it, smiled at it with a kind of distant affection, let it be, as if it were something which had once, in circumstances long since vanished, taken part in his life. A bird flew through his gaze, a shadow engrossed him, the very path, the way it continued and was lost, filled him with a contemplative insight, which seemed to him all the more pure in that he knew he was independent of it. *Where* his usual dwelling place was he couldn't have conceived, but that he was only *returning* to all this here, that he was standing in this body as if in the recess of an abandoned window, looking out:—of this he was for a few seconds so thoroughly convinced that the sudden apparition of one of his friends from the house would have shocked him in the most excruciating way; whereas he truly, deep inside

185

himself, was prepared to see Polyxène or Raimondine or some other long-dead inhabitant of the house step forth from the path's turn. He understood the quiet superabundance of these Things; he was allowed, intimately, to see these ephemeral earthly forms used in such an absolute way that their harmony drove out of him everything else he had learned; he was sure that if he were to move in their midst he wouldn't seem strange to them. A periwinkle that stood near him and whose blue gaze he had already met a number of times, touched him now from a more spiritual distance, but with so inexhaustible a meaning that it seemed as if there were nothing more that could be concealed. Altogether, he was able to observe how all objects yielded themselves to him more distantly and, at the same time, somehow more truly; this might have been due to his own vision, which was no longer directed forward and diluted in empty space; he was looking, as if over his shoulder, *backward* at Things, and their now completed existence took on a bold, sweet aftertaste, as though everything had been spiced with a trace of the blossom of parting. —Saying to himself from time to time that this couldn't last, he nevertheless wasn't afraid that the extraordinary condition would suddenly break off, as if he could only expect from it, as from music, a conclusion that would be in infinite conformity to its own law.

All at once his position began to be uncomfortable, he could feel the trunk, the fatigue of the book in his hand, and emerged. An obvious wind was blowing now in the leaves, it came from the sea, the bushes up the slope were tossing together.

———

Being an artist means: not numbering and counting, but ripening like a tree, which doesn't force its sap, and stands confidently in the storms of spring, not afraid that afterward summer may not come. It does come. But it comes only to those who are patient, who are there as if eternity lay before them, so unconcernedly silent and vast. I learn it every day of my life, learn it with pain I am grateful for: *patience* is everything!

———

I would like to beg you to have patience with everything unresolved in your heart and try to love *the questions themselves* as if they were locked rooms or books written in a very foreign language. Don't search for the answers, which could not be given to you now, because you would not be able to live them. And the point is, to live everything. *Live* the questions now. Perhaps then, someday far in the future, you will gradually, without even noticing it, live your way into the answer.

———

Don't be confused by surfaces; in the depths everything becomes law.

———

What is necessary, after all, is only this: solitude, vast inner solitude. To walk inside yourself and meet no one for hours—that is what you must be able to attain.

———

For one human being to love another human being: that is perhaps the most difficult task that has been entrusted to us, the ultimate task, the final test and proof, the work for which all other work is merely preparation.

———

The future stands still, but we move in infinite space.

———

What we call fate does not come to us from outside: it goes forth from within us.

————

Only someone who is ready for everything, who doesn't exclude any experience, even the most incomprehensible, will live the relationship with another person as something alive and will himself sound the depths of his own being. For if we imagine this being of the individual as a larger or smaller room, it is obvious that most people come to know only one corner of their room, one spot near the window, one narrow strip on which they keep walking back and forth. In this way they have a certain security. And yet how much more human is the dangerous insecurity that drives those prisoners in Poe's stories to feel out the shapes of their horrible dungeons and not be strangers to the unspeakable terror of their cells. We, however, are not prisoners. No traps or snares have been set around us, and there is nothing that should frighten or upset us. We have been put into life as into the element we most accord with, and we have, moreover, through thousands of years of adaptation, come to resemble this life so greatly that when we hold still, through a fortunate mimicry we can hardly be differentiated from everything around us. We have no reason to harbor any mistrust against our world, for it is not against *us*. If it has terrors, they are *our* terrors; if it has abysses, these abysses belong to us; if there are dangers, we must try to love them. And if only we arrange our life in accordance with the principle which tells us that we must always trust in the difficult, then what now appears to us as the most alien will become our most intimate and trusted experience. How could we forget those ancient myths that stand at the beginning of all races, the myths about dragons that at the last moment are transformed into princesses? Perhaps all the dragons in our lives are princesses who are only waiting to see us act, just once, with beauty and courage.

Perhaps everything that frightens us is, in its deepest essence, something helpless that wants our love.

———

I began with Things, which were the true confidants of my lonely childhood, and it was already a great achievement that, without any outside help, I managed to get as far as animals. But then Russia opened itself to me and granted me the brotherliness and the darkness of God, in whom alone there is community. That was what I *named* him then, the God who had broken in upon me, and for a long time I lived in the antechamber of his name, on my knees. Now, you would hardly ever hear me name him; there is an indescribable discretion between us, and where nearness and penetration once were, now distances stretch forth, as in the atom, which the new science conceives of as a universe in miniature. The comprehensible slips away, is transformed; instead of possession one learns relationship, and there arises a namelessness that must begin once more in our relations with God if we are to be complete and without evasion. The experience of feeling him recedes behind an infinite delight in everything that can be felt; all attributes are taken away from God, who is no longer sayable, and fall back into creation, into love and death. It is perhaps only this that again and again took place in certain passages in the Book of Hours, this ascent of God out of the breathing heart—so that the sky was covered with him—, and his falling to earth as rain. But saying even that is already too much.

———

Extensive as the "external" world is, with all its sidereal distances it hardly bears comparison with the dimensions, the *depth-dimensions*, of our inner being, which does not even need the spaciousness of the universe to be, in itself, almost unlimited. It seems to me

189

more and more as though our ordinary consciousness inhabited the apex of a pyramid whose base in us (and, as it were, beneath us) broadens out to such an extent that the farther we are able to let ourselves down into it, the more completely do we appear to be included in the realities of earthly and, in the widest sense, *worldly*, existence, which are not dependent on time and space. From my earliest youth I have felt the intuition that at some deeper cross-section of this pyramid of consciousness, mere *being* could become an event, the inviolable presence and simultaneity of everything that we, on the upper, "normal," apex of self-consciousness, are permitted to experience only as entropy.

Time and space are one; all things are energy; when you move with the speed of light you become infinite: what is this flaky mystic babbling about? Oh, he's a scientist? We knew it all along.

The most beautiful and profound emotion we can experience is the sensation of the mystical. It is the sower of all true science. He to whom this emotion is a stranger, who can no longer wonder and stand rapt in awe, is as good as dead. To know that what is impenetrable to us really exists, manifesting itself as the highest wisdom and the most radiant beauty, which our dull faculties can comprehend only in their primitive forms—this knowledge, this feeling, is at the center of true religion.

———

The scientist's religious feeling takes the form of a rapturous amazement at the harmony of natural law, which reveals an intelligence of such superiority that, in comparison with it, the highest intelligence of human beings is an utterly insignificant reflection. This feeling is the guiding principle of his life and work.

———

The true value of a human being can be found in the degree to which he has attained liberation from the self.

———

A human being is a part of the whole that we call the universe, a part limited in time and space. He experiences himself, his thoughts and feelings, as something separated from the rest—a kind of optical illusion of his consciousness. This illusion is a prison for us, restricting us to our personal desires and to affection for only the few people nearest us. Our task must be to free ourselves from this prison by widening our circle of compassion to embrace all living beings and all of nature.

If you want to see the essence of love, look at the famous photograph of Maharshi. His eyes say it all.

Nobody doubts that he exists, though he may doubt the existence of God. If he finds out the truth about himself and discovers his own source, this is all that is required.

―――

We loosely talk of Self-realization, for lack of a better term. But how can one real-ize or make real that which alone is real? All we need to do is to give up our habit of regarding as real that which is unreal. All religious practices are meant solely to help us do this. When we stop regarding the unreal as real, then reality alone will remain, and we will be that.

―――

Affection toward the good, compassion toward the helpless, happiness in doing good deeds, forgiveness toward the wicked, all such things are natural characteristics of the Master.

―――

If the mind is happy, not only the body but the whole world will be happy. So one must find out how to become happy oneself. Wanting to reform the world without discovering one's true self is like trying to cover the whole world with leather to avoid the pain of walking on stones and thorns. It is much simpler to wear shoes.

―――

Every being in the world longs to be always joyful, without any taint of sorrow. At the same time, everyone loves himself best. Love is caused by joy. Therefore, joy must lie inside oneself. In order to realize this inherent and untainted joy, which indeed we experience every night when the mind is subdued in deep dreamless sleep, it is essential that one know oneself.

———

The ultimate truth is so simple. It is nothing more than being in the pristine state. This is all that need be said.

All religions have come into existence because people want something elaborate and attractive and puzzling. Each religion is complex, and each sect in each religion has its own adherents and antagonists. For example, an ordinary Christian will not be satisfied unless he is told that God is somewhere in the far-off heavens, not to be reached by us unaided. Christ alone knew Him and Christ alone can guide us. Worship Christ and be saved. If he is told the simple truth, that "the kingdom of heaven is within you," he is not satisfied and will read complex and far-fetched meanings into such statements.

Only mature minds can grasp the simple truth in all its nakedness.

———

Question: What are the signs by which one can recognize a true teacher?

Answer: A true teacher is always at home in the depths of the Self. He never sees a difference between himself and others, is never moved by false ideas or distinctions (for example, the idea that he himself is an enlightened sage, that he has realized the truth and attained freedom, while the others around him pine away in bondage and ignorance). His courage and self-control are at all times unshakable. No experience that he encounters can lead him astray.

Question: What qualifications should a true student possess?

Answer: He should have a constant and passionate longing to

194

break free from life's sorrow—not by running away from it, but by growing beyond his mind and thoughts and by experiencing in himself the reality of the Self, which knows neither birth nor death. He should long for the supreme spiritual bliss and have no other desires.

———

Reality is simply the loss of the ego. Destroy the ego by seeking its identity. It will automatically vanish and reality will shine forth by itself. This is the direct method.

There is no greater mystery than this, that we keep seeking reality though in fact we *are* reality. We think that there is something hiding reality and that this must be destroyed before reality is gained. How ridiculous! A day will dawn when you will laugh at all your past efforts. That which will be on the day you laugh is also here and now.

———

People often say that a liberated Master should go out and preach his message to the people. How can anyone be a Master, they argue, as long as there is misery by his side? This is true. But who is a liberated Master? Does he see misery beside him? They want to determine the state of a Master without realizing the state themselves. From the standpoint of the Master their contention amounts to this: A man dreams a dream in which he finds several people. On waking up, he asks, "Have the dream people also woken up?" How ridiculous!

In the same way, a good man says, "It doesn't matter if I never get liberation. Or let me be the last man to get it so that I may help all others to be liberated before I am." Wonderful. Imagine a dreamer saying, "May all these dream people wake up before I do." The dreamer is no more absurd than this amiable philosopher.

———

Silence is a perennial flow of language, interrupted by words. It is like electricity. When there is resistance to its passage, it glows as a lamp or revolves as a fan. But in the wire it remains as pure energy. In the same way, silence is the eternal flow of language.

———

God's grace is the beginning, the middle, and the end. When you pray for God's grace, you are like someone standing neck-deep in water and yet crying for water. It is like saying that someone neck-deep in water feels thirsty, or that a fish in water feels thirsty, or that water feels thirsty.

Between being lost and being found, there is the consciousness of being lost: the only true agony, as when a foot that was asleep begins to wake up.

There are two main human sins from which all others derive: impatience and indolence. Because of impatience they were expelled from Paradise, because of indolence they don't return. But perhaps there is only one main sin: impatience. Because of impatience they were expelled, because of impatience they don't return.

———

Beyond a certain point there is no return. This point has to be reached.

———

The crows assert that a single crow could destroy the heavens. This is certainly true, but it proves nothing against the heavens, because heaven means precisely: the impossibility of crows.

———

Idleness is the beginning of all vices, the crown of all virtues.

———

The Messiah will come only when he is no longer necessary.

———

In the struggle between yourself and the world, second the world.

———

With the strongest light one can dissolve the world. Before weak eyes it becomes solid, before still weaker eyes it grows fists, before still weaker eyes it becomes shamefaced and smashes anyone who dares to look at it.

———

There are questions that we wouldn't be able to get over if we weren't by our very nature set free from them.

———

The fact that there is nothing but a spiritual world deprives us of hope and gives us certainty.

———

Not a drop overflows, and there is no room for a single drop more.

———

The fact that our task is exactly as large as our life makes it appear infinite.

———

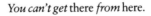

You can't get there *from* here.

If the place I want to arrive at could only be reached by a ladder, I would give up trying to arrive at it. For the place I really have to reach is where I must already be.

What is reachable by a ladder doesn't interest me.

———

The solution of the problem that you see in life is to live in a way that will make what is problematic disappear.

The fact that life is problematic means that your life doesn't fit into life's shape. So you must change your life, and when it fits into the shape, what is problematic disappears.

But don't we have the feeling that someone who doesn't see a problem in life is blind to something important, to the most important thing of all? Don't I want to say that someone like this is just going along with his life—blindly, like a mole, and if only he could see, he would see the problem?

Or shouldn't I say rather: that whoever lives rightly, experiences the problem not as *sorrow*, and therefore not problematic, but rather much more as a joy; therefore, so to speak, as a bright halo around his life, not as a questionable background.

———

The mystical is not *how* the world is, but *that* it is.

———

I can well imagine a religion in which there are no doctrines, so that nothing is spoken. Clearly, then, the essence of religion can have nothing to do with what is sayable.

The truth can be spoken only by someone who already lives inside it; not by someone who still lives in untruth and only sometimes reaches out from untruth toward it.

When does God create heaven and earth? In the beginning. And when is the beginning? At every moment. Dying to past and future, we are born into the creative Now. Beginner's mind is the mind of God.

Our "original mind" includes everything within itself. It is always rich and sufficient within itself. You should not lose your self-sufficient state of mind. This does not mean a closed mind, but actually an empty mind and a ready mind. If your mind is empty, it is always ready for anything; it is open to everything. In the beginner's mind there are many possibilities; in the expert's mind there are few.

———

When we practice zazen, our mind always follows our breathing. When we inhale, the air comes into the inner world. When we exhale, the air goes out to the outer world. The inner world is limitless, and the outer world is also limitless. We say "inner world" or "outer world," but actually there is just one whole world. In this limitless world, our throat is like a swinging door. The air comes in and goes out like someone passing through a swinging door. If you think, "I breathe," the "I" is extra. There is no you to say "I." What we call "I" is just a swinging door which moves when we inhale and when we exhale. It just moves; that is all. When your mind is pure and calm enough to follow this movement, there is nothing: no "I," no world, no mind or body; just a swinging door.

———

To live in the realm of Buddha nature means to die as a small being, moment by moment. When we lose our balance we die, but at the same time we also develop ourselves, we grow. Whatever we see is changing, losing its balance. The reason everything looks beautiful is because it is out of balance, but its background is always in perfect harmony. This is how everything exists in the realm of Buddha nature, losing its balance against a background of perfect balance.

———

The big mind in which we must have confidence is not something which you can experience objectively. It is something which is always with you, always on your side. Your eyes are on your side, for you cannot see your eyes, and your eyes cannot see themselves. Eyes only see things outside, objective things. If you reflect on yourself, that self is not your true self any more. You cannot project yourself as some objective thing to think about. The mind which is always on your side is not just your mind, it is universal mind, always the same, not different from another's mind.

———

We must have beginner's mind, free from possessing anything, a mind that knows everything is in flowing change. Nothing exists except momentarily in its present form and color. One thing flows into another and cannot be grasped. Before the rain stops we hear a bird. Even under the heavy snow we see snowdrops and some new growth. In the East I saw rhubarb already. In Japan in the spring we eat cucumbers.

Every time we say "Thy will be done," we should have in mind all possible misfortunes and all possible blessings, because a blessing may be more difficult to accept than a misfortune. Better yet, we should have in mind nothing at all.

In what concerns divine things, belief is not appropriate. Only certainty will do. Anything less than certainty is unworthy of God.

———

Perfect and infinite joy really exists within God. My participation can add nothing to it, my non-participation can take nothing from the reality of this perfect and infinite joy. Of what importance is it then whether I am to share in it or not? Of no importance whatever.

———

To desire in the void, to desire without any wishes. To detach our desire from all good things and to wait. Experience proves that this waiting is satisfied. It is then that we touch the absolute good.

———

The good seems to us as a nothingness, since there is no *thing* that is good. But this nothingness is not unreal. Compared with it, everything in existence is unreal.

———

Every time that we say "Thy will be done," we should have in mind all possible misfortunes added together.

———

God continually showers the fullness of his grace on every being in the universe, but we consent to receive it to a greater or lesser extent. In purely spiritual matters, God grants all desires. Those who have less have asked for less.

––––––

If we find fullness of joy in the thought that God exists, we should find the same fullness in the knowledge that we ourselves do not exist, for it is the same thought.

––––––

It is not for man to seek, or even to believe in, God. He only has to refuse his ultimate love to everything that is not God. This refusal does not presuppose any belief. It is enough to recognize what is obvious to any mind: that all the goods of this world, past, present, and future, real or imaginary, are finite and limited and radically incapable of satisfying the desire that perpetually burns within us for an infinite and perfect good.

––––––

Until God has taken possession of him, no human being can have faith, but only simple belief; and it hardly matters whether or not he has such a belief, because he will arrive at faith equally well through disbelief.

––––––

Absolutely unmixed attention is prayer.

Translated by Emma Craufurd

BIOGRAPHICAL AND
BIBLIOGRAPHICAL NOTES

Abu Sa'id ibn Abi'l-Khayr Fadlallah ibn Muhammad al-Mayhani (967–1049), Persian mystic and poet. After an early period of asceticism, the service of the poor became his spiritual practice; he begged food for the poor, swept their mosques, cleaned their toilets. "The shortest way to God," he once said, "is to bring comfort to the soul of your neighbor."

Abu Yazid Tayfur ibn 'Isa ibn Surushan al-Bistami (?–c. 874), Persian mystic, founder of the ecstatic school of Sufism.

Once a disciple of Dhu'l-Nun knocked on the door of Abu Yazid's cell. The Master said, "Whom are you looking for?" The disciple said, "Abu Yazid." The Master said, "Who is Abu Yazid, and where is he? I have been seeking Abu Yazid for a long time, but I haven't found him." When the disciple returned to Dhu'l-Nun and told him what had happened, Dhu'l-Nun said, "My brother Abu Yazid is lost with those who are lost in God."

Bakhya ibn Pakuda (1040–1110), Spanish rabbi.

The Bible (7th?–3rd? century B.C.E.). These dates refer to the final versions; some material in the Bible dates from the 11th century B.C.E. and before.

Blake, William (1757–1827), English visionary, poet, and artist. A prophet in a rationalistic age, Blake was considered insane during his lifetime and was neglected for nearly a century afterward.

"Men are admitted into Heaven," he wrote, "not because they have curbed & govern'd their Passions or have No Passions, but because they have Cultivated their Understandings. The Treasures of Heaven are not Negations of Passion, but Realities of Intellect, from which all the Passions Emanate Uncurbed in their Eternal Glory."

See the wonderful contemporary account of him in *The Portable Blake* (Viking, 1946), pp. 675 ff. Henry Crabb Robinson, the diarist, a conventional Englishman who met Blake several times, with a hilarious mixture of condescension, bafflement, and interest, said that "in the sweetness of his countenance and gentility of his manner he added an indescribable grace to his conversation," and described an early visit thus: "Everything in the room squalid and indicating poverty, except

himself. And there was a natural gentility about him, and an insensibil-
ity to the seeming poverty, which quite removed the impression. Besides, his linen was quite clean, his hand white, and his air quite unem-
barrassed when he begged me to sit down as if he were in a palace." At
one point Blake said to him, "I cannot think of death as more than the
going out of one room into another." Elsewhere Crabb Robinson
wrote, "I put the popular question to him, concerning the imputed divinity of Jesus Christ. He answered: 'He is the only God'—but then he
added—'And so am I and so are you.'"

The Buddha, Siddhartha Gautama (c. 563–c. 483 B.C.E.), Indian monk,
teacher, and religious reformer. His enlightenment occurred as he was
sitting under the Bodhi tree; according to the Mahayana tradition,
when he saw the morning star he exclaimed, "Marvelous! Marvelous!
All beings are already enlightened! It is only because of their delusions
that they don't realize this."

Chuang-tzu (369?–286? B.C.E.), Chinese Taoist Master, philosopher, and
comedian.

Probably the most famous passage in his book is the following: "Once
Chuang-tzu dreamt that he was a butterfly, fluttering around, happy
with himself and absolutely carefree. He didn't know he was Chuang-
tzu. Suddenly he woke up: there he was in the flesh, unmistakably
Chuang-tzu. But he didn't know if he was Chuang-tzu who had just
dreamt that he was a butterfly, or a butterfly now dreaming that he was
Chuang-tzu."

See *The Way of Chuang-tzu*, by Thomas Merton, New Directions,
1965, and *The Complete Works of Chuang-tzu*, translated by Burton
Watson, Columbia University Press, 1968.

The Cloud of Unknowing (mid- to late 14th century), written by an anonymous English monk sometime between 1349 and 1395.

See *The Cloud of Unknowing*, translated into modern English with an
introduction by Clifton Wolters, Penguin, 1961.

Dhu'l-Nun al-Misri, Abu'l-Fayd Thawban ibn Ibrahim (796–861), Egyptian mystic, called "the head of the Sufis." His father was a Nubian
slave.

Someone once asked Dhu'l-Nun, "When does the Sufi reach his goal?"
He said, "When he is as he was where he was before he was."

The Diamond Sutra (4th? century), written in India; the greatest of the Mahayana Buddhist scriptures. According to tradition, the famous Sixth

Founding Teacher of Zen, Hui-neng, when he was a poor peasant boy selling firewood in the market, became enlightened upon hearing this sutra for the first time.

See *The Diamond Sutra and The Sutra of Hui Neng*, translated by A. F. Price and Wong Mou-Lam, Shambhala, 1969.

Dōgen Kigen (1200–1253), Japanese Zen Master, philosopher, poet, painter, founder of the Soto Zen school in Japan. His first religious experience occurred when he was seven years old, according to his earliest biographer: "At the loss of his beloved mother, his grief was intense. As he saw the incense-smoke ascending in the Takao temple, he recognized the transitoriness of all things. Thereby the desire for enlightenment was awakened in his heart." His most important work is the *Shobo-genzo* (*Treasury of the True Dharma Eye*), a collection of discourses and sermons in ninety-five fascicles.

"The Manifestation of the Truth" ("Genjokoan") has the following note appended to it: "Written in mid-autumn, 1233, and given to my lay student Koshu Yo of Kyushu. Revised in 1252."

See *Moon in a Dewdrop*, edited by Kazuaki Tanahashi, North Point Press, 1985, *How to Raise an Ox*, by Francis H. Cook, Center Publications, 1978, and *The Sound of Valley Streams*, by Francis H. Cook, State University of New York Press, 1989.

Dov Baer of Mezritch (?–1772), Ukrainian rabbi, called "the Great Maggid (Preacher)," disciple of the founder of Hasidism, the Baal Shem Tov. A visitor once said of Dov Baer, "I didn't travel to Mezritch to hear him teach, but to see how he tied his shoelaces."

Once Shmelke of Nikolsburg asked Dov Baer to explain the Talmudic commandment that we should praise God for evil as much as we praise him for good. Dov Baer said, "Go to the House of Study and ask my student Zussya." Shmelke went to the House of Study and found Zussya: emaciated, filthy, clothed in rags. Shmelke asked, "How can we praise God for evil as much as we praise him for good?" "I can't tell you," said Zussya, "because nothing bad has ever happened to me."

Eckhart, Meister Johannes (1260–1327), German priest and theologian, the greatest of Christian teachers. His views were condemned as heretical by Pope John XXII.

See *Breakthrough: Meister Eckhart's Creation Spirituality in New Translation*, Introduction and Commentaries by Matthew Fox, O.P., (translations by Robert Cunningham, Ron Miller, Matthew Fox, Elizabeth Heptner, and Thomas O'Meara), Doubleday, 1980, and *Meister Eckhart, German Sermons and Treatises*, translated with introduction and notes by M. O'C. Walshe, vols. 1 and 2, Watkins, 1979, 1981.

Einstein, Albert (1879–1955), German-Jewish physicist and Zionist.

Emerson, Ralph Waldo (1803–1882), American essayist and poet.

Erigena, Johannes Scotus (c. 810–c. 877), Irish theologian.

Fa-tsang (643–712), Chinese philosopher, Third Founding Teacher of the Flower Garland School of Buddhism.

See *Entry Into the Inconceivable: An Introduction to Hua-yen Buddhism*, by Thomas Cleary, University of Hawaii Press, 1983.

al-Ghazali, Abu Hamid Muhammad ibn Muhammad al-Tusi (1058–1111), Persian Sufi, theologian, jurist, religious reformer; said to be the most famous of all Muslim writers.

The Gospel of Thomas (1st–2nd century), a collection of sayings attributed to Jesus. Fragments of the original Greek text were discovered in Egypt at the turn of this century, and a Coptic translation of the complete text turned up in 1945, along with other important Gnostic manuscripts. The Gospel of Thomas contains material, from very early Church traditions, which is not preserved in the four official Gospels. Some of the sayings seem to be genuine sayings of Jesus.

See *The Nag Hammadi Library in English*, edited by James M. Robinson, Harper & Row, 1977.

Gregory of Nyssa (c. 331–395), Cappadocian bishop and theologian, one of the four great fathers of the Eastern Church.

I am sorry to report that Gregory, elaborating on such vicious language as Matthew 27:25, John 8:44, and 1 Thessalonians 2:14f., called the Jews "Lord-killers," "fighters against God," "God-haters," and "advocates of the devil." He was evidently far from "purifying the heart of every destructive passion."

Heraclitus (6th–5th century B.C.E.), Greek philosopher.

The Hermetic Writings (3rd century), a collection of short essays and dialogues by Egyptian philosophers of the neo-Platonic school.

Huang-po Hsi-yun (?–849), Chinese Zen Master, disciple of Pai-chang and teacher of Lin-chi; said to be seven feet tall, with a large pearl-shaped lump in the middle of his forehead.

See *The Zen Teaching of Huang Po*, translated by John Blofeld, Grove Press, 1958, and *Original Teaching of Ch'an Buddhism*, translated by Chang Chung-yuan, Pantheon, 1969.

Hugh of St. Victor (c. 1100–1141), German philosopher and theologian.

Hui-hai Ta-chu (8th century), Chinese Zen Master, disciple of Ma-tzu (709–788).

When Hui-hai first came to Ma-tzu, the Master asked him, "What have you come here for?" Hui-hai said, "I have come seeking the Buddha's teaching." "What a fool you are!" Ma-tzu said. "You have the greatest treasure in the world inside you, and yet you go around asking other people for help. What good is this? I have nothing to give you." Hui-hai bowed and said, "Please, Master, tell me what this treasure is." Ma-tzu said, "Where is your question coming from? *This* is your treasure. It is precisely what is asking the question at this very moment. Everything is stored in this precious treasure-house of yours. It is there at your disposal, you can use it as you wish, nothing is lacking. You are the master of everything. Why then are you running away from yourself and seeking for things outside?" Upon hearing these words, Hui-hai realized his own mind. Beside himself with joy, he bowed deeply to the Master.

Later, when Ma-tzu first read the manuscript of Hui-hai's *Treatise on the Essential Gateway to Truth by Means of Instantaneous Awakening*, he said, "In Yueh Chou there is now a great pearl; its luster penetrates everywhere freely and without obstruction." Because of this, Hui-hai became known as the Great Pearl.

See *The Zen Teaching of Hui Hai*, translated by John Blofeld, Rider & Company, 1962.

Isaac of Nineveh (6th century), Syrian monk and hermit.

Jesus of Nazareth (4? B.C.E.–30? C.E.), Jewish prophet, healer, and religious reformer.

Thomas Jefferson, a particularly insightful reader of the Gospels, said about him:

> His parentage was obscure, his condition poor, his education null, his natural endowments great, his life correct and innocent; he was meek, benevolent, patient, firm, disinterested, and of the sublimest eloquence. . . . Among the sayings and discourses imputed to him by his biographers, I find many passages of fine imagination, correct morality, and of the most lovely benevolence; and others again of so much ignorance, so much absurdity, so much untruth, charlatanism, and imposture, as to pronounce it impossible that such contradictions should have proceeded from the same being. . . . [If we wish to know about Jesus, we must read] the simple Evangelists; select, even from them, the very words only of Jesus, paring off the amphibolog-

isms into which they have been led by forgetting often, or not understanding, what had fallen from him, by giving their own misconceptions as his dicta, and expressing unintelligibly for others what they had not understood themselves. There will be found remaining the most sublime and benevolent code of morals which has ever been offered to man.

John the Evangelist (1st–2nd century), unknown author writing in Ephesus, Antioch, or Alexandria. Traditionally the Gospel and Epistles of John and the Book of Revelations are ascribed to the apostle John son of Zebedee, but modern scholarship dates the books considerably later. The Epistles were probably, and Revelation certainly, not written by the author of the Gospel.

Julian of Norwich, Dame (1343–?), English anchoress; there is evidence that she was still alive in 1416. Her revelations took place in 1373, and she received further insight into them in 1393.

See *Revelations of Divine Love*, translated into modern English with an introduction by Clifton Wolters, Penguin, 1966.

Kafka, Franz (1883–1924), Czech-Jewish novelist and short-story writer.
See *Dearest Father: Stories and Other Writings*, translated by Ernst Kaiser and Eithne Wilkins, Schocken Books, 1954.

Kuei-shan Ling-yu (771–853), Chinese Zen Master; co-founder, with his disciple Yang-shan, of the Kuei-Yang school of Zen.

Kuei-shan once asked Yang-shan, "In the forty volumes of the Nirvana Sutra, how many words come from the Buddha and how many from demons?" Yang-shan said, "They are all demons' words." Kuei-shan said, "From now on, no one will be able to pull the wool over your eyes."
See *Original Teaching of Ch'an Buddhism*, translated by Chang Chung-yuan, Pantheon, 1969.

Maneri, Sharafuddin Ahmad ibn Yahya (1263–1381), Indian Sufi, called "The Spiritual Teacher of the Realm." He wrote more than two hundred confidential letters, over a twenty-five-year period, to his chief disciple and successor, Muzaffar Shams Balkhi; Muzaffar, however, ordered that they be buried with him, except for one small bundle of twenty-eight letters.

See *Sharafuddin Maneri: The Hundred Letters*, translation, introduction, and notes by Paul Jackson, S.J., Paulist Press, 1980.

Maximus of Tyre (125–185), Greek rhetorician and philosopher.

Montaigne, Michel Eyquem de (1533–1592), French essayist.

Emerson said of him, "Montaigne is the frankest and honestest of all writers. . . . The sincerity and marrow of the man reaches to his sentences. I know not anywhere the book that seems less written. It is the language of conversation transferred to a book. Cut these words, and they would bleed; they are vascular and alive."

Muhammad (570?–632), Arabian prophet and religious reformer; the founder of Islam.

al-Muhasibi, Abu 'Abdallah al-Harith ibn Asad (?–857), Arabian Sufi and theologian.

Novalis (1772–1801), nom de plume of Friedrich von Hardenberg, German poet, metallurgist, and aphorist. His greatest work, the long, fragmentary Encyclopedia (still untranslated into English), is filled with fascinating connections and insights about poetry, physics, women, art, philosophy, religion, mathematics, history, ethics, magic, cosmology, philology, psychology, physiology, and love.

Padmasambhava (8th century), Indian monk. At the invitation of the king of Tibet, he brought Buddhism from India to Tibet in 747. According to tradition, he buried his sacred texts in the hills of central Tibet, where they were later discovered by Karma-Lingpa, an incarnation of one of his disciples. His ancient biographer says that he died in 858 at the age of three thousand.

See *The Tibetan Book of the Dead*, a new translation with commentary by Francesca Fremantle and Chögyam Trungpa, Shambhala, 1975, and *The Tibetan Book of the Great Liberation*, translated by W. Y. Evans-Wentz, Oxford University Press, 1954.

Pai-chang Huai-hai (720–814), Chinese Zen Master, teacher of Huang-po and of Kuei-shan, who said of him, "He is majestic and dignified, brilliant and luminous. His is the soundlessness before sound and the colorlessness after the pigment has faded. He is like an iron bull: when a mosquito lands on him it can't find a place to sting."

Pai-chang was the founder of the Zen monastic schedule of physical labor and meditation. Dōgen writes, "Pai-chang was at the extreme of old age, and on occasions of 'all-invited' work, when everybody labored vigorously, the whole assembly felt pain and regret that their old teacher should be included in the work party. Finally some monks hid his tools and would not hand them over. That day Pai-chang refused to eat, as compensation for not using mattock and bamboo basket. He said, 'A day of no work is a day of no eating.' "

See *Sayings and Doings of Pai-chang*, translated by Thomas Cleary, Center Publications, 1978.

Philo (c. 20 B.C.E.–c. 50 C.E.), Jewish-Alexandrian Platonic philosopher and Biblical exegete.

Plato (428–348 B.C.E.), Greek philosopher and poet.

Ramana Maharshi (1879–1950), Indian sage ("Maharshi" means "great sage"), perhaps the greatest spiritual teacher of the twentieth century. He was well known for treating all visitors with equal courtesy, whether they were squirrels or maharajahs. Gandhi used to send burnt-out followers of his to Maharshi for spiritual refreshment.

His enlightenment experience occurred when he was sixteen years old:

> About six weeks before I left Madura for good, the great change in my life took place. It was quite sudden. I was sitting alone in a room on the first floor of my uncle's house. I was rarely sick, and on that day there was nothing wrong with my health, but I was seized by a sudden, violent fear of death. There was nothing in my state of health to account for it, and I didn't try to account for it or to find out whether there was any reason for the fear. I just felt "I am going to die" and began thinking what to do about it. It didn't occur to me to consult a doctor or my elders or friends; I felt that I had to solve the problem myself, there and then.
>
> The shock of the fear of death drove my mind inward and I said to myself mentally, without actually speaking the words, "Now death has come; what does it mean? What is it that is dying? This body is dying." And I at once dramatized the occurrence of death. I lay down with my limbs stretched out stiff as though rigor mortis had set in and imitated a corpse so as to give greater reality to the inquiry. I held my breath and kept my lips tightly closed so that no sound could escape, so that neither the word "I" nor any other word could be uttered. "Well then," I said to myself, "this body is dead. It will be carried stiff to the burning ground and there burnt and reduced to ashes. But with the death of this body am I dead? Is this body I? It is silent and inert, but I feel the full force of my personality and even the voice of the 'I' within me, apart from it. So I am Spirit transcending the body. The body dies, but the Spirit that transcends it cannot be touched by death. That means I am the deathless Spirit." All this was not dull thought; it flashed through me vividly as living truth; I perceived it directly, almost without thought-process. "I" was something very real, the only real thing about my present state, and all the conscious activity connected with my body was centered on that "I." From that moment onward the "I" or Self focussed attention on itself by a powerful fascination. Fear of

death had vanished at once and forever. Absorption in the Self continued unbroken from that time on. Other thoughts might come and go like the various notes of music, but the "I" continued like the monotone *sruti* note that underlies and blends with all the other notes. Whether the body was engaged in talking, reading, or anything else, I was still centered on "I." Previous to that crisis I had no clear perception of my Self and was not consciously attracted to it. I felt no perceptible or direct interest in it, much less any inclination to dwell permanently in it.

See *Ramana Maharshi and the Path of Self-Knowledge*, by Arthur Osborne, Weiser, 1973, *Be As You Are: The Teachings of Sri Ramana Maharshi*, edited by David Godman, Arkana, 1985, *Talks with Sri Ramana Maharshi*, by Munagala S. Venkataramiah (6th edition), Sri Ramanasramam, 1978, *Letters from Sri Ramanasramam*, by Suri Nagamma, Sri Ramanasramam, 1973, and *Day by Day with Bhagavan*, by A. Devaraja Mudaliar, Sri Ramanasramam, 1968.

Rilke, Rainer Maria (1875–1926), German-language poet, widely acknowledged as the greatest poet of our century. The central event of his life occurred in 1912, when a voice spoke to him the beginning lines of the great *Duino Elegies*. Rilke had to wait until 1922 for their completion; in three weeks, caught up in "a hurricane of the spirit," as if taking dictation, often "in a single breathless obedience," he wrote down the last five Elegies, the fifty-four *Sonnets to Orpheus*, and additional poems and prose.

See *The Selected Poetry of Rainer Maria Rilke*, Random House, 1982, *The Notebooks of Malte Laurids Brigge*, Random House, 1983, *Letters to a Young Poet*, Random House, 1984, and *The Sonnets to Orpheus*, Simon & Schuster, 1985, all translated by Stephen Mitchell.

Rumi, Jelaluddin (1207–1273), Sufi mystic and poet, born in what is now Afghanistan; founder of the Mevlevi, the ecstatic dancing order known in the West as the Whirling Dervishes. In 1244 he met the wandering dervish Shams al-Din ("the Sun of Religion") of Tabriz, an overwhelming experience that led Rumi into the depths of divine love.

Rumi's habits of composition were described by his beloved disciple Husam:

> He never took a pen in hand. He would recite wherever he was: in the dervish college, at the Ilgin hot springs, in the Konya baths, in the vineyards. When he started, I would write, and I often found it hard to keep up with his words. Sometimes he would re-

cite day and night for several days. At other times, he wouldn't compose for months. Once for a period of two years he didn't speak any poetry. As each volume was completed, I would read it back to him, so that he could revise it.

See *Open Secret*, versions by John Moyne and Coleman Barks, Threshold Books, 1984, *Unseen Rain*, Quatrains of Rumi by John Moyne and Coleman Barks, Threshold Books, 1986, *We Are Three*, New Rumi translations by Coleman Barks, Maypop Books, 1987, *These Branching Moments*, translated by John Moyne and Coleman Barks, Copper Beech Press, 1988, *This Longing, Poetry, Teaching Stories, and Letters of Rumi*, translated by Coleman Barks and John Moyne, Threshold Books, 1988, *Delicious Laughter: Rambunctious Teaching Stories from the Mathnawi*, versions by Coleman Barks, Maypop Books, 1990, *Like This*, versions by Coleman Barks, Maypop Books, 1990, and *When Grapes Turn to Wine*, versions by Robert Bly, Yellow Moon Press, 1986.

Sa-Go-Ye-Wat-Ha, a.k.a. Red Jacket (1752–1830), orator and chief of the Wolf tribe of the Senecas; his name means "He-Keeps-Them-Awake."

Seattle, Chief (1786–1866), chief of the Suquamish, Duwamish, and allied Salish-speaking tribes, born near present-day Seattle. Chief Seattle's speech, given at a tribal gathering on January 9, 1855, was directed to Isaac Stevens, the first governor of the new Washington Territory, in response to an offer from President Franklin Pierce to buy Indian lands in the Northwest and provide a reservation for Seattle's people and other tribes. After Seattle signed the Point Elliott Treaty in the spring of 1855, war broke out, but eventually most of his people settled on reservation land.

Seattle is described as follows in a contemporary account by Dr. Henry A. Smith: "He was the largest Indian I ever saw, and by far the noblest looking. He stood nearly six feet in his moccasins, was broad-shouldered, deep-chested, and finely proportioned. His eyes were large, intelligent, expressive, and friendly. He might have been an emperor, but all his instincts were democratic, and he ruled his subjects with kindness and paternal benignity." According to another contemporary account, "When he addressed his people, he could be heard by listeners even at a distance of three-quarters of a mile—such was the resonance and carrying power of his voice."

Shankara (686–718), Indian yogi and philosopher, the founder of Advaita Vedanta, the fundamental principle of which is that the only reality is

God. It is said that he had written many commentaries on the Hindu scriptures by the age of ten.

One morning, shortly after Shankara's enlightenment experience in his early teens, as he was on his way to bathe in the Ganges, he met an Untouchable on the path. Caste prejudice arose, and Shankara, the Brahmin, ordered him aside. But the Untouchable said, "If there is only one God, how can there be many kinds of men?" Filled with shame and reverence, Shankara prostrated himself before the Untouchable. This incident inspired one of his most famous poems; each of its five stanzas ends with the refrain:

> He who has learned to see the one Reality everywhere,
> He is my master—whether he is a Brahmin or an Untouchable.

See *Shankara's Crest-Jewel of Discrimination*, translated by Swami Prabhavananda and Christopher Isherwood, Vedanta Press, 1947.

Shmelke of Nikolsburg (?–1778), Moravian rabbi.

Shmelke was famous for his charity; every beggar who knocked at his door was given a coin, even if this left Shmelke's family without enough to eat. Once Shmelke had no money, so he gave a beggar a ring. "What have you done now?" his wife said. "That ring cost four hundred ducats!" Shmelke ran out the door, caught up with the beggar, and said, "Listen, that ring is worth four hundred ducats. Don't let them swindle you when you sell it."

Spinoza, Baruch (1632–1677), Dutch-Jewish philosopher and Biblical scholar. For a hundred years after his death he was considered a pernicious atheist. He was discovered for European culture by Lessing; Goethe fell in love with his *Ethics*; and Novalis called him "a God-intoxicated man." According to Bertrand Russell, he is "the noblest and most lovable of the great philosophers."

See *The Collected Works of Spinoza, vol. 1*, edited and translated by Edwin Curley, Princeton University Press, 1985, and *Works of Spinoza*, translated by R. H. M. Elwes, vols. 1 and 2, Dover Publications, 1951, 1955.

Suzuki, Shunryu (1905–1971), Japanese Zen Master, and one of the first authentic Buddhist teachers to live in the West.

See his *Zen Mind, Beginner's Mind*, Weatherhill, 1970.

Symeon the New Theologian (949–1022), Greek Orthodox abbot and poet, born in Paphlagonia (northern Turkey). His discourses, which aimed at leading his monks into a greater awareness of God's presence within them, stirred up fierce opposition in the local archbishop and among the official theologians, and in 1009 he was exiled to a small town on the Asiatic shore of the Bosporus, where he spent the rest of his life.

Thoreau, Henry David (1817–1862), American writer and naturalist.

Traherne, Thomas (1637–1674), English priest and poet. The anonymous manuscripts of his *Poetical Works* and *Centuries of Meditation* were found in a bin of a London bookshop in 1895. After some skillful literary detective work by the editor and critic Bertram Dobell, the manuscripts were traced to Traherne, an obscure Anglican clergyman. When the poems were published in 1903, and the *Centuries* in 1908, they caused a literary sensation.

Tu-shun (557–640), Chinese philosopher, First Founding Teacher of the Flower Garland School of Buddhism.

See *Entry Into the Inconceivable: An Introduction to Hua-yen Buddhism*, by Thomas Cleary, University of Hawaii Press, 1983.

Tzu-ssu (483–402 B.C.E.), philosopher, grandson of Confucius. The passages I have selected come from the Chung Yung (*The Central Harmony*, or, as Ezra Pound translates it in his very quirky version, *The Unwobbling Pivot*), which is traditionally ascribed either to Tzu-ssu or to Confucius' disciple Tseng-tzu.

See *The Wisdom of Confucius*, translated by Lin Yutang, Modern Library, 1938.

The Upanishads (8th?–5th? century B.C.E.), along with the Bhagavad Gita, the central texts of the Hindu religion. Traditional Indian scholars date them around 1500 B.C.E.

See *The Ten Principal Upanishads*, put into English by W. B. Yeats and Shree Purohit Swami, Macmillan, 1937, and *The Upanishads*, translated by Eknath Easwaran, Nilgiri Press, 1987.

Weil, Simone (1909–1943), French-Jewish philosopher, theologian, sociologist, and political activist.

Wittgenstein, Ludwig (1889–1951), Austrian-Jewish philosopher.

Wu-men Hui-k'ai (1183–1260), Chinese Zen Master, author of the most widely used koan textbook.

See *The Gateless Barrier*, by Robert Aitken, North Point Press, 1991.

Yehiel Mikhal of Zlotchov (?–c. 1786), Polish rabbi, disciple of the founder of Hasidism, the Baal Shem Tov.

He once said, "Pray for your enemies that everything may be well with them. More than all other prayers, this is truly the service of God."

Yuan-wu K'e-ch'in (1063–1135), Chinese Zen Master, author of the introductions, remarks, and commentaries to *The Blue Cliff Record*, a collection of one hundred koans originally compiled by Hsueh-tou Ch'ung-hsien (980–1052). Yuan-wu's most famous successor, Ta-hui, destroyed the book's printing blocks; he thought that Zen students were so captivated by the beauty of its language that it had become an obstacle to enlightenment.

See *The Blue Cliff Record*, translated by Thomas and J. C. Cleary, Shambhala, 1977.

Yun-men Wen-yen (?–949), Chinese Zen Master. He forbade his monks to take notes on his talks: "Why should you preserve my speech," he said, "and tie up your own tongues?" It is only thanks to the ingenuity of his attendant, Hsiang-lin, who dressed in a paper robe and surreptitiously recorded the Master's words, that a few of the talks have come down to us.

A monk once asked Yun-men, "What is the essence of Buddhism?" Yun-men said, "When spring comes, the grass grows by itself."

Another time a monk asked, "What is it like to swallow the truth in one gulp?" Yun-men said, "I will be inside your belly."

Yun-men's most famous answer was to a monk who asked him, "What is Buddha?" Yun-men said, "Dry shit on a stick."

See *Original Teaching of Ch'an Buddhism*, translated by Chang Chung-yuan, Pantheon, 1969.

A NOTE ON THE TRANSLATIONS

All translations and adaptations in this book are mine, unless otherwise indicated.

With the Hebrew, Greek, Latin, and German texts I worked from the original languages. Sources for other versions are as follows:

The Upanishads: W. B. Yeats and Shree Purohit Swami, Eknath Easwaran, Swami Prabhavananda and Frederick Manchester, Swami Nikhilananda.

The Buddha: I. B. Horner, Nyanatiloka, David Maurice, and Maurice Walshe.

Tzu-ssu: Yi-pao Ming, Lin Yutang, and Ezra Pound. I have also taken a sentence from Gary Snyder's poem "Axe Handles."

The Gospel of Thomas: Thomas O. Lambdin and Marvin W. Mayer.

The Diamond Sutra: A. F. Price and Edward Conze.

Muhammad: Abu Bakr Siraj Ed-Din.

Pai-chang, Kuei-shan, and Yun-men: Chang Chung-yuan, *Original Teachings of Ch'an Buddhism*, Pantheon, 1969.

Hui-hai: *The Zen Teaching of Hui Hai*, translated by John Blofeld, Rider & Co., 1962.

Padmasambhava: W. Y. Evans-Wentz, *The Tibetan Book of the Great Liberation*, Oxford University Press, 1954.

Huang-po: *The Zen Teaching of Huang Po*, translated by John Blofeld, Grove Press, 1958.

Bakhya ibn Pakuda: The old Hebrew translation of the original Arabic.

Dōgen: Robert Aitken and Kazuaki Tanahashi, Thomas Cleary, and Francis H. Cook.

Eckhart: I have consulted Josef Quint's translation into modern German.

Montaigne: In (slightly) revising the Hazlitt revision, I have adopted a few words and phrases from the Donald M. Frame translation. The translation of the verses from Horace (Odes I, xxxi, 17–20) is my own.

Spinoza: I have consulted the Elwes, Wolf, and Curley translations.

Sa-Go-Ye-Wat-Ha: William L. Stone, *The Life and Times of Red Jacket, or Sa-Go-Ye-Wat-Ha*, Wiley and Putnam, 1841.

I have made minor changes in several of the other translations for the sake of consistency.

Chief Seattle: Adapted by William Arrowsmith from the Victorian English version of Dr. Henry A. Smith, which was published in the Seattle *Star* on October 29, 1887. (There is another, widely distributed version of this speech which makes it into a plea for ecology; William Arrowsmith calls it "a heavily tendentious and much-expanded version; in fact, a contemporary forgery.")

"The great chief Washington": The Indians believed that Washington was still alive, perhaps because they confused the name of the city with the name of the "reigning chief." [William Arrowsmith's note]

"The White Chief's son": Governor Stevens. [W. A.]

"King George": The Indians believed King George III was still on the English throne. [W. A.]

"has moved his boundary northward": A reference to the Oregon Compromise of 1846, redefining the boundaries between the United States and British Columbia. [W. A.]

Verse numbers of the selections from the Bible, Jesus, Thomas, and John:
"And God looked . . .": Genesis 1:31.
"Jacob was left alone . . .": Genesis 32:24ff.
"Moses said . . .": Exodus 3:13f.
"You shall love the Unnamable . . .": Deuteronomy 6:5ff.
"Love your neighbor . . .": Leviticus 19:18.
"For this pattern . . .": Deuteronomy 30:11ff.
"And he said, 'Go and stand . . .'": I Kings 19:11.
"I form light . . .": Isaiah 45:7.
"I will put my truth . . .": Jeremiah 31:33ff.
"He has made everything beautiful . . .": Ecclesiastes 3:11.
"Be still . . .": Psalm 46:10.
"You have hidden the truth . . .": Psalm 51:6.
"Love your enemies . . .": Matthew 5:44f.
"Don't be anxious . . .": Matthew 6:25ff.
"Ask, and it will be given to you . . .": Matthew 7:7.
"Unless you change your life . . .": Matthew 18:3.
"Don't judge . . .": Luke 6:37f.
"There once was a man . . .": Luke 15:11ff.
"The kingdom of God does not come . . .": Luke 17:20f.

"Jesus said, 'If your teachers . . .' ": The Gospel of Thomas 3.

"Jesus said, 'Recognize . . .' ": Thomas 5.

"Jesus said, 'When you see . . .' ": Thomas 15.

"The disciples said to him, 'Tell us what . . .' ": Thomas 18.

"Jesus saw some infants nursing . . .": Thomas 22.

"Jesus said, 'Blessed are those . . .' ": Thomas 49.

"The disciples said to him, 'When will the repose . . .' ": Thomas 51.

"Jesus said, 'Whoever believes . . .' ": Thomas 67.

"Jesus said, 'If you bring forth . . .' ": Thomas 70.

"Jesus said, 'I am the light . . .' ": Thomas 77.

"The disciples said to him, 'Tell us who . . .' ": Thomas 91.

"The disciples said to him, 'When will the kingdom . . .' ": Thomas 113.

"In the beginning . . .": John 1:1.

"To all who receive him . . .": John 1:12.

"And you shall know the truth . . .": John 8:32.

"The spirit you have received from him . . .": 1 John 2:27.

"Love comes from God . . .": 1 John 4:7.

"Behold, I make all things new . . .": Revelation 21:5f.

ACKNOWLEDGMENTS

For their helpful suggestions, I am indebted to William Arrowsmith, Coleman Barks, Dan Gerber, Burt Jacobson, Jack Kornfield, Herbert Mason, Daniel Matt, Michael Roche, Donald Sheehan, and Huston Smith.

The idea of the brief prefaces came from Michael Katz, my agent: for which, as for so much else, I am grateful.

And, of course, to Vicki.